With the Guards during the Peninsular War, 1805-14

VOLUME 1

ALEXANDER GEORGE FRASER, LORD SALTOUN

IN LATER LIFE

With the Guards during the Peninsular War, 1805-14

VOLUME 1

The Campaigns of the First (later Grenadier) Guards
and Letters of a Serving Officer, Alexander Fraser,
Lord Saltoun

ILLUSTRATED

John H. Lewis

LEONAUR

With the Guards during the Peninsular War, 1805-14
VOLUME 1
The Campaigns of the First (later Grenadier) Guards and Letters of a Serving Officer,
Alexander Fraser, Lord Saltoun
by John H. Lewis

ILLUSTRATED

First published as part of *The March to Hougoumont:* August 2020

Leonaur is an imprint of Oakpast Ltd

The author, John H Lewis asserts his rights for copyright purposes
© 2025 Oakpast Ltd

ISBN: 978-1-916535-98-5 (hardcover)
ISBN: 978-1-916535-99-2 (softcover)

http://www.leonaur.com

Publisher's Notes

Contents

Introduction to the Revised Editions

I trust that the following lines are not the first the reader has encountered that reveal that this book constitutes approximately half of the pages of a book that I wrote, which was first published in 2020, titled, 'The March to Hougoumont'. I have done my best in the description on this book's cover and in marketing descriptions to ensure that would not be the case.

I confess I was quite pleased with that title at the time that it was constructed, because I believed it had a nice ring to it and the conception of that book came about—quite literally—during a personal tour of the château-farm of Hougoumont on the Waterloo battlefield in Belgium.

The book that came to being tracked the career of a notable personality of that engagement—a British Army officer, Alexander Fraser, Lord Saltoun—and combined it with a narrative of his regiment—The First (later Grenadier) Guards during the years of its participation in the campaigns against Napoleonic France from 1805 to 1815.

At the risk of confessing to vanity, I was quite pleased with the outcome of that endeavour, so I was initially comparatively surprised that the book—given it contained a great deal of original information and was (so far as I knew) the only comprehensive modern book which recounted the history of the Grenadier Guards during that period—did not appeal to as wide a readership as I imagined it justifiably might.

Upon later reflection I realised why that may have been the case. As a matter of fact, I should not have made these errors in the first instance, because this was not the first occasion, I had personally made similar mistakes in the publishing of books!

The first error was that I was so engaged with the project that the finished text eventually ran to 437 published pages, which had its inevitable consequence on the costs of its print production and so, inevitably, on the price of the book to the consumer.

My second error was that my choice of title placed the subject material squarely on the field of Waterloo. This famous battle certainly has its enthusiastic students, but the fact is the engagement at Hougoumont appears towards the closing part of the initial 437-page book, though before the stand of the First Guards on the ridge at Waterloo and, therefore, certainly before the actions that were fought by that regiment on the road to Paris in 1815. So Saltoun's experiences at Hougoumont did not even constitute a climax of that general theme.

Much of the initial parts of that book concern the regiment during the Peninsular War and indeed during the disastrous action on Walcheren. Clearly, in the minds many readers of military history, the Peninsular War and the Campaign of 1815 are quite a different and distinct subjects, notwithstanding that both the book's principal character and his regiment were continually active throughout this period.

So, I decided to remedy both of these shortcomings by re-issuing this text in two shorter volumes—each with an unambiguous title—so that readers might purchase which part most interests them and in so doing gain a cost advantage into the bargain.

The splitting point of the original text worked conveniently well, since it appears at the time of the so called, 'Sortie from Bayonne', which, as most students of the period know, strictly speaking tragically occurred after the conclusion of the Peninsular War (which constitutes the majority of the first volume) in 1814. Indeed, the emperor had abdicated the throne three days prior to that futile blood-letting. So, volume two—ultimately leading to the 'Hundred Days'—begins with a brief description of the final campaign of the First Empire of the French.

Finally, this initiative enabled me to remedy a typographic error which had been annoying me for four years! I have retained the original introduction and acknowledgements in each volume for context.

JHL 2024

Introduction by the Author

Converging paths. Intersecting events and lives. These are the weft and warp of the fabric of history. Some are momentous in their effects, some are seemingly insignificant, but all are interdependent and in their connections are carried the destinies of the affairs of humankind.

This book, of course, concerns only a very small portion of that huge and fascinating cloth. It is the story of a premier infantry regiment of the British Army; the First Regiment of Foot Guards, which in due course became the Grenadier Guards, during a particularly active and significant period of its own long and illustrious history. It is also the story of a young man who joined that regiment and served with it as an officer growing in experience and distinction as his career progressed, principally revealed in this book through his journals and correspondence.

It is a story of wars and campaigns which have become among the most notable among the history of the warfare of comparatively modern times for they were fought, from the perspective of that soldier and his regiment, against the First Empire of the French under the inspirational leadership of one of the most outstanding military figures in history, the Emperor Napoleon. He created an epoch, the spirit of which has endured to perennially fascinate historians and, of course, it therefore inevitably concerns the military career of the Duke of Wellington, who became the emperor's nemesis. It also transpired to be, perhaps quite unexpectedly from the author's perspective, a love story.

These elements were inexorably drawn together, travelling for a decade on roads that ran through Sicily, Iberia, France and the Low Countries until they eventually arrived at a cataclysmic rendezvous during which, over a three day period between the 16th and 18th of June, 1815, were fought two of the most renowned engagements in the annals of conflict; The Battle of Quatre Bras and The Battle of Waterloo.

Our principal character, having seen long service during the Peninsular War and other conflicts, fought in both of those battles, in part commanding two light companies of the First Guards tasked with the defence of the orchard and wood of Hougoumont. This *château*-farm had been transformed into a bastion and was the key of the extreme right of Wellington's defensive line, so had essentially to be held against the attacking French troops under the command of Napoleon's brother, Prince Jerome Bonaparte, to prevent a flanking manoeuvre in that direction. He then took his place with his regiment, in its principal position and with it withstood the great cavalry charges against the beleaguered squares of infantry, thereafter playing his part in the final action of the battle which brought the Imperial Guard to ruin.

How the book you are holding came into being is another story of converging lines and intersecting events, though it is, of course, a far more prosaic tale. That said it is one worth the telling, for it is not without some interest. The beginning of that story came about not long after two hundred years had elapsed from the time of the Battle of Waterloo though, quite genuinely, on the field of that very conflict in the farmlands beyond the city of Brussels in Belgium.

Since it remains a working farm in private ownership the ordinary visitor can (at the time of writing) only safely gaze wistfully at the buildings of the farm of La Haye Sainte, in front of the centre of the British line, from the other side of a usually busy road. Likewise, Hougoumont was until recently privately owned and although there was access to it for special interest groups, for most of my time, as a very ordinary visitor, one could not enter this legendary position which became, 'a battle within the battle'.

My wife and partner, Patsie and I (in company with one of our grandsons) visited the newly renovated Hougoumont, now at last open to the public, at the first opportunity available to us. This is not the place to describe Hougoumont or the engagement that was fought there, for that will eventually appear in the course of this book. In any event that first visit, for us, was less about historical detail than about atmosphere. We were, simply put, overwhelmed to be walking on the cobbles and within the space of such iconic, evocative and familiar events. It is true that one can experience similar sensations practically anywhere on the field of Waterloo, but these impressions are surely nowhere (currently accessible) more profound than within Hougoumont.

The paintings of the scenes of the battle for Hougoumont have long been very familiar to those who have an interest in military art and these events. Hillingford's scene in the courtyard, Dighton's action beyond the south gate, Gibb's iconic image of the north gate being shouldered shut by the Guards as the French infantry try to burst through and perhaps above all, for me, Ernest Crofts' wonderful painting from the perspective of the attacking French infantry. Brutal and appalling as all warfare undeniably is, it is virtually impossible not to be romantically swept away under the influence of these images (which was the idea of them, of course) when one stands upon the locations, readily and infallibly identifiable, where these dramas took place.

Since the Hougoumont visitor centre curators have constructed steps and a wooden platform for the purpose, Patsie and I found our way to the defenders' side of the garden wall beyond the south gate, which appears to the right of Crofts' painting and, returning in the imagination two hundred years, peering over it for a moment, indulged in our reveries. That moment was short lived.

It was a warm afternoon and so we were both wearing short-sleeved shirts, our forearms resting on the brick parapet. Before long, an extraordinarily large flying insect, not immediately identifiable to us, but attired in the yellow and black striped uniform ominously associated with wasps, flew up to Patsie, boldly alighted on one of her exposed arms and without preamble, slowly extended a long 'bayonet' from its nether region, presumably with the intention of sinking it into her flesh. It had selected entirely the wrong target.

Not one to panic, a familiar (to me, anyway) expression of combined vexation and determination crossed over my wife's usually pleasant countenance. The creature was then promptly and decisively 'batted for six' by Mrs. Lewis with a severe, 'Get off, you *blank!*' reprimand to accompany a really impressive trajectory as it spiralled away to cross some far away boundary. I laughed aloud, the gravitas of the history of the place notwithstanding, since, unbidden, it immediately occurred to me this was not the first time an affronted English voice had said those words at that point, on that wall with much the same outcome. Whilst Patsie is some way (and many inches) from a guardsman of any era, I had read similar phrases several times spoken by British soldiers upon different battle-grounds in various campaigns among the many personal military narratives that have come my way.

It was then, believe it or not as you will, that I began to contemplate how a book could be created that included the struggle for Hougoumont in a way that had not necessarily been covered before by other writers within other books. This does not admittedly amount to much by way of serious academic motivation for the creation of a work of history, but we are in the business of making books in quantity and one inspiration or epiphany serves fairly as well as any other. So, there it is.

My first thoughts for the model of the enterprise were not so very far from the kind of book that has ultimately come to fruition. That was it should combine the career of one of the notable personalities of the Guards who fought in the Battle of Waterloo in or around Hougoumont, within a narrative that embraced his own regiment's service during the Napoleonic Wars; a march which inexorably led to Hougoumont and, as it transpired, beyond.

When I considered the potentials of Lord Saltoun (pronounced Salton), by the time of Waterloo, a 30-year-old captain/lieutenant-colonel of the Third Battalion, First Guards, initial investigations were not promising. I knew nothing about him other than in accounts of the action at Hougoumont in which his name appeared regularly so I apologise if, in the light of what follows, my ignorance seems peculiar to the better informed. There did not seem to have been a biography published concerning his life. He had not written an autobiography, so far as I could discover, nor indeed a published volume of recollections confined to his military career. It then occurred to me that Saltoun, since it is a title, might not necessarily be the name under which such a volume might have been written. Lord Saltoun, (the 16th of that title, incidentally) was in fact Alexander George Fraser of the Fraser's of Philorth.

I began, therefore, to make further investigations in that direction which was when, in the parlance of those who dig in hope of discovering treasure, 'I hit pay-dirt', for another Alexander Fraser, (the 17th Lord Saltoun and our subject's nephew) had served posterity particularly well by becoming the author, archivist and presumably publisher (since the work is a privately circulated, numbered limited edition from 1879) of a substantial three volume work chronicling the extraordinarily long history of his Scottish family and there, to keep this introduction no longer than it need be and to avoid repetition, in volume three was the correspondence of his uncle, written during his service with the First Guards (and latterly Grenadier Guards) in the course of the Napoleonic wars and, of course, including the Waterloo Campaign. I subsequently discovered more valuable biographical material was included in volume one.

It may be that this correspondence has been published elsewhere specifically within the context of these campaigns, but I can only report that if that is the case, then in the course of my fairly extensive reading on this subject, it has slipped by me. So, this was a 'Eureka' moment. Indeed, my enthusiasm was about to exponentially increase, since my first recourse was to investigate the number of Peninsular War bibliographies in my possession and, having done so, found within them no reference to these letters. This was reassuring for discoveries like this do not come one's way very often or in my case, more accurately, to this date, ever.

So, I was thrilled and motivated for I had found my subject or, dependent on one's perspective, it had found me. That pleasure was enhanced by the fact that Alexander Fraser, Lord Saltoun was no stranger to the section of wall and garden that had inspired the creation of a book that became this book. Converging paths and intersecting events had become a theme. What agency sent the intersecting insect responsible for all of this, I cannot say nor dare venture to speculate. All the afore written is true though, I do assure you, as indeed to the best of my ability to judge and relate, is what follows.

John H. Lewis, 2020

Acknowledgements

My first acknowledgements must be that I am not an academic of history or any other subject and I have never been a soldier. I do not profess, likewise, to be an expert on the subject of the Peninsular War or indeed the Waterloo Campaign, notwithstanding that I can honestly claim to have read many works on both subjects for pleasure, as an editor and as a publisher. My own career was in the media, firstly as a journalist followed by several decades in creative marketing. So, my first instinct as an author is to entertain by telling a good story and my hope is that, in its company, the reader will spend some rewarding and pleasurable time. I have ploughed through my share of books on interesting historical subjects, crammed with essential, well researched information which were, nevertheless, something of an endurance course to read, much less complete. Their authors did not, demonstrably, have the recreation of others highly placed on their agendas. However, from my own perspective, my worst disservice in the recounting of Saltoun's fascinating and eventful story would be that I made it appear dull.

That I have employed Lord Saltoun's papers published within, 'The Frasers of Philorth', published in three volumes by Alexander Fraser, The 17th Lord Saltoun, printed in Edinburgh for private circulation in 1879, may be acknowledged with little emphasis, since he is the principal character in this story and these papers were not only the inspiration for this book, but also comprise a significant portion of its content. I have also been extensively guided by 'The Origins & History of the First or Grenadier Guards', by Lieutenant-General Sir F.W Hamilton in three volumes published by John Murray, London in 1871. Hamilton was formerly a Grenadier Guards officer, who served actively with the regiment during the Crimean War.

I am persuaded—on the whole—that it is reliable to follow the detail provided in these kinds of books, written in the nineteenth century, as to matters concerning regimental movements etc., because the authors certainly have had access to regimental records and diaries together with memoirs and manuscripts. In Hamilton's case, he may have been able to speak directly with some of the people who took part in the events here related or to their immediate families, since he was born in 1815—in fact, just 10 days before the Battle of Waterloo was fought.

One cannot take the entire contents of these kinds of volumes as completely dependable for several reasons. They invariably reveal a bias on the part of their authors with regard to their principal subjects, since these kinds of books (this one, as revealed, being no exception) are frequently written by former members of the regiment in question. So not only can they be guaranteed to contain only favourable views of their subjects, but one may discover that more emphasis has been placed on the role of the regiment or regimental individuals than may have been—in sober judgement—the case. This habit also tends to minimise or relegate to obscurity those who were also involved in the same events, but who were not associated with the author's regiment. For example, Hamilton's account of the conflict for Hougoumont does not mention the name of the officer in command of the post who was not a First Guard, but, at the time, a Coldstreamer. Since that omission cannot be ascribed to any other account on the subject, one must consider MacDonnell's absence from Hamilton's narrative to be intentional. In fact, there are a number of differences between Daniel Mackinnon's account of the Coldstreams at Hougoumont and the Grenadier Guards' history on the same subject by Hamilton.

I have taken some pains to briefly mitigate these kinds of shortcomings, for without doing so it is impossible for the reader to have an understanding of all the events which were taking place in the same location and period of time. That having been said, the First Guards (later Grenadier Guards) do intentionally appear in this book as the particular focus and perspective, because it is not intended to be a general history of the events featured within it and Saltoun was always, during this period of his life, an officer of that regiment and their stories are, therefore, inextricably entwined.

Secondly, the authors of these kinds of books have a tendency to be diplomatic to the point of servility concerning the influential characters of society who appear in their pages, whether for reasons of good form or self-preservation, it is difficult to evaluate; something of both factors was probably the case, though for the historical record, accuracy and candour are the perpetual casualties. If the better-informed reader discovers that I have failed to be diligent with regard to any of those erroneous assertions that required rectification, then I offer my unreserved apologies.

It was also never my intention to deal with battles and campaigns fully in military detail—orders of battle, casualties etc. In fact, I have also deliberately only sketched the assault on Bergen-op-Zoom in 1814, because only a small number of First Guards were actually involved in the assault itself and Saltoun was not involved at all. Similarly, events in the Peninsular War that did not include the Guards are only mentioned in their chronological place. A work which embraced all of these details would be huge and the thread of the intended narrative would have been inevitably submerged.

That kind of information is available, in any event, elsewhere so I decided, in the interests of keeping matters simple and the book something smaller than the dimensions of a house brick, to take my military and political cues, concentrating on the 'broad brush-strokes' in the main, from the extremely thorough and accessible writings of Professor Charles Oman and Sir John Fortescue. I have supplemented these with reference to Captain William Siborne's invaluable, 'History of the War in France and Belgium in 1815,' (Fourth Edition) T & W Boone, London, 1848 and, of course, his collated 'Waterloo Letters' written by British officer participants in some of these events and collated into book form by his son, since in these, it seems to me, will be found information—closest coming from 'the horse's mouth'—which has the likelihood of being both authentic and comparatively accurate.

That having been said, one can never be entirely certain of these matters concerning events two centuries in the past, of course, so where there have been inconsistencies I have undertaken some further research from various other sources including Daniel Mackinnon's, 'Origin & Services of the Coldstream Guards', Volume 2, Richard Bentley, London, 1833. The author was present within Hougoumont during the battle. Similarly, and for the same reason, I have accessed Rees Howell Gronow's anecdotes which appeared in several volumes of reminiscences and recollections.

Gronow was an officer of the First Guards who served during the Peninsular War and during the Campaign of 1815. He was within the regimental position at Waterloo and on the march thereafter to Paris and he brings a sensitive, humane and occasionally humorous aspect to these events. Of course, as a brother officer, he knew Saltoun well, enabling the reader to see him as others saw him and I have valued his contribution more from the perspective of his impressions than his accurate reportage of the military facts. I have discovered several other letters and journal extracts written by First Guards and have utilised them at points in the narrative for much the same reason as the inclusion of the Gronow extracts.

Common accord is, however, often hard to find, as anyone who has cross-referenced a quantity of written history very well knows. Definitive 'truth', in my view, stands on a peak too steep for me to scale and too tenuous to stand upon indefinitely, even if one reaches the summit. So, I make no claims of planting my flag upon it. Rather than coming to conclusions in those cases where broad agreement remains elusive, I have assumed the role of an impartial reporter of versions rather than misrepresenting myself as a new authority.

Nevertheless, I have been unable to resist the selfish temptation to editorialise and that is because notions have occurred to me in the course of my extensive reading of different versions of the same events during the period covered by this book and indeed, as a consequence of editing both Oman's and Fortescue's writings on the Napoleonic era . If I am in error or provoke disagreement in those instances where I have let my opinions or imagination run free, I have only my own hubris to blame, which as anyone who is likely to read this book knows, is a time-honoured cause of personal downfall.

It is traditional to thank people who have given assistance on these kinds of projects and, whilst I trust I am given to a generosity of spirit, I cannot make a list of mine very long for Leonaur is a small publishing imprint and we keep pretty much to ourselves. Everyone associated with it knows who they are and what they contribute to it. They also know what I feel about them, because we are in the most part related in one way or another or have been comrades for a long time.

I must, on behalf of Leonaur, acknowledge the contribution made by the graphic designer and artist, Glyn Staves, in the creation of the illustrations of Hougoumont. It has been my privilege to know and work with Glyn for many years in several capacities including, in this case, as his client. It is worth emphasising that the motivation behind the commission of this 3D image was to give the reader an *impression* of the *château*-farm and its environs. It is also intended to assist in the identification of the locations of events which took place around the buildings, roads and pathways, gardens, orchards and woods, described in the text. We have achieved that objective by the examination of a plethora of available material (including satellite images) and, where there were gaps of information we could not readily fill, we have employed some considered imagination and artistic licence. The author is well aware of the significant volume of serious research that has been undertaken at the site and which, indeed, is ongoing at time of writing. Though proportions and relative distances are more or less accurate, these illustrations were never intended to be considered in a remotely academic way. However, in keeping with the spirit that guided the writing of this story I trust, since I have seen nothing quite like them myself in the past, that perusing them will give others some enjoyment.

Two other people stand clear in my mind and they are Charles 'Charlie' Radford, former C.O of the 16th/5th Lancers and the veteran historian, Ian Robertson. Both men have always made me feel we were doing something worthwhile. So, thank you both, that encouragement has always been appreciated, whether you were aware you were giving it or not. In Charlie Radford's case he must also be thanked for eliciting approvals and assistance from the families of several authors whose work we have published and so, accordingly, all of those very kind people must be thanked for their open-hearted generosity and cooperation. Finally, I must acknowledge the support of everyone who has purchased a Leonaur imprint book, most especially Kevin Jones who has, to date, diligently collected every Leonaur Napoleonic subject title in a hardback edition.

J. H. L

CHAPTER ONE

Lord Saltoun & His Regiment

The First Guards (today and as of 1815, The Grenadier Guards) regiment was raised by Charles II in 1656 as Lord Wentworth's Royal Regiment of Guards, whilst he was in exile in Bruges, in modern Belgium, following the English Civil War, which was, at that time, within the Spanish held Netherlands. The regiment first went into action at the Battle of the Dunes, near Dunkirk in 1658. This was a peculiar baptism of fire since the royalist regiment, among Spanish allies, was fighting not only the French under Turenne, but also their allies; troops from the British Commonwealth under Lockhart. The battle was a French victory and the soldiers who had remained loyal to their king suffered severely. However, their time of exile was soon to come to an end and the survivors accompanied Charles II to England in 1660 upon the restoration of the monarchy following Oliver Cromwell's death and the collapse of the Commonwealth.

During the remainder of the 17th century the regiment saw its share of action, fighting in the capacity of marines aboard Royal Navy ships during the Dutch Wars 1665-7, most notably off Lowestoft and in the Battle of Sole Bay. It was during this period that John Churchill (later the Duke of Marlborough) joined the regiment as an ensign.

More conventional infantry service followed at Tangier on the North African, Mediterranean coast (which had come to Charles II as part of the dowry of his wife, the Portuguese princess, Catharine of Braganza) against the Moors in 1680. Notwithstanding the English king's claims, made without their consent and probably their knowledge, the local inhabitants took some exception to the incursive presence of *infidels* on their lands and hostilities inevitably broke out. The Guards were awarded their first battle honour, 'Tangier', for their service, which was also the first battle honour (Honorary Distinction) of the modern British Army.

The Battle of Sedgemoor in 1685 saw the regiment fighting on English soil to defeat, Charles II's illegitimate pretender son, the rebellious Duke of Monmouth. Foreign service came again in Flanders during the War of the League of Augsburg, 1689-97, though matters did not begin auspiciously for the regiment, which suffered a defeat at the Battle of Steenkirk in 1692 and again in 1693 at the Battle of Landen. The assault of the fortress of Namur in 1695 brought about a restoration of the regiment's fortune for the enemy position was successfully carried, a French Marshal was captured, and 'Namur' became the regiment's second battle honour.

With the first years of the 18th century came a new war against the French which brought to the fore the superlative generalship of the Duke of Marlborough, placing him in the pantheon of his nation's outstanding military men. During the War of Spanish Succession, 1701-14, the First Guards initially saw action at the fortified hill-top position of The Schellenberg, overlooking Donauworth, in July,1704. This desperate action cost the lives of three quarters of the First Guards grenadiers who led the assault, though the battle delivered Marlborough his first victory of the campaign and gave the French their first battlefield defeat in approaching half a century. The renowned victory at the Battle of Blenheim followed in the following month and, during the subsequent five years of the war, the regiment added battle honours which resound to this day including, 'Ramillies', 1706, 'Oudenard', 1708 and 'Malplaquet', 1709. Additionally, between 1704-5, 200 soldiers of the First Guards successfully contributed to the defence of Gibraltar earning the regiment yet another battle honour for its colours.

Another issue of European royal succession created a pretext for war and once again the British Army was in conflict with the old enemy; the France of the Bourbons. The War of Austrian Succession, 1740-48, brought forth two notable engagements which involved the First Guards. The first was the Battle of Dettingen, 1743 which was the last occasion a British monarch commanded on the field of battle. The second was the Battle of Fontenoy, 1745; a hard-fought affair which was probably concluded in a stalemate, but is not regarded as a British victory since the French force held the field of conflict at the close of the engagement.

Meanwhile, the Jacobite Rebellion was breaking out in Scotland. Guards were employed on horseback as mounted infantry to move swiftly northwards and although four hundred First Guards assisted in the relief of Carlisle, they did not take part in the final battle on Culloden Moor which brought the aspirations of Charles Stuart and his highlanders to ruin. The regiment suffered defeat in the abortive Raid on St. Malo on the northern coast of France, 1758 and, despite gallant service, in the disastrous (for the British cause) American War of Independence, 1775-83.

★★★★★★

The Frasers of Philorth are a lowland Scottish family whose clan chieftains are representative peers of Scotland; the Lords Saltoun. The family seat is Castle Fraser at Sauchen in Aberdeenshire and they should not be confused, therefore, with the highland Frasers of Lovat, centred about Inverness. The first Lord Saltoun, in the fifteenth century, was Lawrence Abernethy and there followed nine Abernethy, Lords Saltoun in succession until the seventeenth century when Margaret Abernethy became the 10th Lord Saltoun. However, her position is not traditionally counted and thus, henceforth a Lord Saltoun could be referred to as (for example) the 17th and the 16th Lord Saltoun. From Margaret Abernethy the title transferred to the Fraser family name and to date, eight Lords Saltoun have borne Alexander as their Christian name.

MARJORY FRASER, LADY SALTOUN
WIFE OF THE FIFTEENTH LORD ÆTAT INTER 80 - 90
DIED NOV 15TH 1881, ÆTAT 9?

ALEXANDER FRASER,
FIFTEENTH LORD SALTOUN.
BORN 1785. DIED 1793

By the closing decades of the 18th century war with the old enemy, France, was again looming. This enemy was no longer, of course, the France of the Bourbons for the age of revolution had dawned, the head of the Bourbon king, Louis XVI had fallen into the basket of the guillotine in Paris in January, 1793. The established orders of continental Europe were then under no illusion that they entering into a period of dire instability and threat.

In the same year, the early and unexpected death of the fifteenth (by traditional styling) Alexander Fraser, Lord Saltoun, in September 1793, meant his eldest son, Alexander George Fraser, the subject of this narrative, who was born on the 22nd of April 1785, succeeded to the title when he was between eight and nine years of age. In this book he is principally referred to as Saltoun, since that is the name, he used himself, even when corresponding to close family members. The impact of the loss of a father on a young boy requires no elaboration, though he, of course, received the abiding support of his mother, Margery and that of his maternal grandfather, Simon Fraser of Ness Castle.

★★★★★★

The French Revolutionary Wars, 1793-1802 heralded more than a contest for territory and resources, for the tricolour of republicanism championed an ideology which proposed to eradicate the power of monarchs, aristocracies and the church wherever it could prevail.

In the first year of the war the First Guards, as part of a small force of just over a thousand troops under the command of General Gerard Lake, (who would earn laurels in India against the Marathas in concert with the soldier who would one day become the Duke of Wellington), marched upon the fortified hill-top village of Lincelles in Flanders which was occupied by 5,000 of the enemy. The successful assault, against artillery and massed musket fire, was carried out with great gallantry and in consequence, 'Lincelles' was awarded to the First Guards as another battle honour.

★★★★★★

Alexander Fraser was sent to the public school at Eton, where, as an extraordinarily bold and fit young man, he soon earned a reputation among his schoolfellows for deeds of daring. He was the first Etonian to jump into the Thames from the parapet of the centre arch of Windsor Bridge. A junior contemporary said that he remembered, upon first attending Eton, that the whole school was 'ringing with the description of a fight that had just taken place between Lord Saltoun and a champion of the bargemen', or *bargees* as they were termed. The young Saltoun apparently triumphed on that occasion. In another encounter with the *bargees* he had a very narrow escape, for tripped up by the prone body of a friend, he fell on his back whereupon one of the *bargees* stabbed at him with a pitchfork. He was found stunned by the fall, but uninjured, the prongs having passed, one on each side of his neck, pinning him into the ground.

★★★★★★

Six years after Lincelles was fought, in 1799, the First Guards took part in their final campaign of the century in the expedition to the Helder. Against all expectations, and much to the surprise of all those who opposed it, the inexperienced army of the new republic of France frequently fared well on the field of conflict. France's determination to spread republicanism throughout Europe had, by this time, already created six minor republics including the Batavian Republic of Holland and Belgium. The great powers including Russia, Austria, Prussia and Britain determined to decisively defeat the French revolutionary armies, for they were by this time, thinly spread whilst engaged in several campaigns and so considered to be particularly vulnerable. The Second Coalition of nations to oppose France was formed and hostilities commenced, delivering some initial success for the allies, principally because they possessed significant numerical superiority.

A joint Russian and British force was formed for an expedition to the Low Countries to ensure the French concentrated defences on a hitherto unthreatened frontier. The plan was then to capture a number of valuable military arsenals, the ships of the

Dutch naval fleet and re-establish the power of the Stadtholder. Furthermore, it was hoped that the people of the new republic (including those under arms in the service of the enemy) would stand aside from the conflict and, in due course, join the allies. The campaign was launched by a landing in North Holland near to the Helder since this location provided a secure anchorage for the fleet and placed the army within striking distance of Amsterdam.

Poor weather delayed the landing giving notice of its arrival to the French, who could see the invasion force at sea, allowing them the time to concentrate their own forces. The landing transpired to be unopposed, but the advance guard had hardly begun to move forward before it was hotly engaged by the enemy. Nevertheless, the Helder was secured, the enemy garrison withdrew and two line-of-battle ships, five frigates and thirteen Indiamen immediately fell into British hands. The Dutch navy crews, as had been hoped, refused to fight, which soon delivered more valuable enemy vessels into the hands of the invaders.

The campaign on land, before long however, began to founder and the British commander, Abercromby, aware that the terrain between his force and the enemy was latticed with canals and ditches would not risk an advance until he was reinforced. His counterpart, Brune, perceiving his opponent's procrastination, struck pre-emptively, employing his entire force on the 10th of September. Two brigades of Guards under Burrard were well placed to defend the village of Pettin on the left of the line and despite being sorely pressed threw back the attacking force, inflicting losses of approaching 1,000 men, whilst suffering very few casualties themselves. Burrard's career, alas, would not continue so promisingly.

Soon after this action the Duke of York arrived with reinforcements and assumed command of the British Army which, in concert with its Russian allies, began an advance towards Bergen. The minute details of this brief and entirely unsuccessful campaign are not germane to the principal theme of this account, though it is worth noting that from a position of strength the allies very soon found themselves at such a disadvantage that not only was success acknowledged as impossible, but a fighting evacuation was also considered untenable. The Duke of York therefore entered into negotiations with the republicans which would allow the unhindered departure of his command and this arrangement was ratified towards the end of October. Sir James Pultney, the final senior British officer to depart from the continental shore, embarked with his last remaining troops on the 19th November, 1799. The French re-occupied the Helder on the same day.

The turn of the new century was just weeks away and Revolutionary France was making its presence and potentials felt in ways that guaranteed the nineteenth century would, for the coalition nations, begin in strife and uncertainty which showed very little indication of abating or improving. Indeed, by the close of the same year, the brilliant General Napoleon Bonaparte had, following a short military career, risen in power to establish himself as the First Consul of France.

★★★★★★

In 1802, at seventeen years old, Lord Saltoun entered the British Army, receiving his commission of ensign (by purchase) in the 91st, (Argyllshire Highlanders) Regiment of Foot in which his uncle, Major General Duncan Campbell of Lochnell, held the rank of colonel. By the Autumn of the same year he had become a lieutenant in the second battalion of the 35th Regiment of Foot which at that time bore the territorial title of 'Dorsetshire', (it was retitled the 35th (Sussex) Regiment of Foot in 1805) and from which he was put on half-pay in 1803 when the battalion was reduced. Subsequently he obtained a lieutenancy in the 42nd Highlanders, The Black Watch, remaining in that regiment until he attained the rank of captain in 1804, when, on the 23rd of November, he exchanged into the First Regiment of Foot Guards. In the British Army the First Guards was, among the infantry and household regiments of foot, the pinnacle of the military elite and a fitting regiment in which to serve for a young man of Saltoun's social status.

★★★★★★

Such was Napoleon's meteoric rise in power that by 1805 he had crowned himself Emperor of France. The nations of Europe had only just begun to see the consequences of this remarkable man's lust for power which would dominate politics and embroil them in war on the continent for another turbulent decade. In England, the young Saltoun was initially established in the First Battalion, First Guards, but in January 1805 he was transferred to the third battalion, with which he took the first steps of his military career on active service abroad and with which he would during his time with the regiment, henceforth, be associated.

CHAPTER TWO

The Expedition to Sicily, 1805–1807

Since the regiment's service during the expedition to the Helder, no battalions of the First Guards had been sent for service overseas. The government's priority had been the safety of Britain and the security of its coastline from an expected invasion by the French. So, the maintenance of military resources at close quarters to oppose such an incursion, should it arise, entirely influenced the deployment of the regiment during the first years of the nineteenth century. However, in 1805, the third and first battalions, First Guards, were selected to be part of the reinforcements sent to the Mediterranean island of Sicily.

For the purposes of this narrative, the Expedition to Sicily is significant, though it has, together with the peculiar battle of Maida in Calabria on the Italian 'toe peninsula' (July 4th 1806) with which it is associated, taken a subordinate position in the complete account of Britain's campaigns against France at this time. In France, the Revolution and Consulate periods had come to an end and Britain was about to embark on the long wars with the First Empire of the French under the autocratic influence of Napoleon Bonaparte. Furthermore, it was from Sicily that the first of Saltoun's letters, which form the focus of this account, were written and despatched to his family.

Nelson's great final naval victory off Cape Trafalgar in October 1805, had established the Royal Navy's dominance in sea-power to the extent that Napoleonic France could never again aspire to compete with the British anywhere on the seas and oceans. Indeed, the Royal Navy ruled the waves in the absence of any serious challenge from any nation for over a century, until the Battle of Jutland during the First World War. At the turn of the 18th and 19th centuries however, the double blow of the Battle of the Nile, (1798) and the subsequent Battle of Trafalgar, meant the Royal Navy effectively controlled the waters of the Mediterranean Sea, which was of vital significance, strategically and logistically, for nations at war across continental Europe.

Perhaps more importantly for immediate events, the Royal Navy's blockade of the English Channel neutralised the French, 'Army of the Ocean Coast', or as it was more optimistically titled, 'The Army of England', waiting to invade Britain from its camps around Boulogne in Northern France. Once again, and not for the last time, the English Channel, though not wide in miles, demonstrated itself to be quite wide enough. As a French invasion of Britain ceased to be a viable proposition for him, Napoleon, never done with his machinations, turned his attentions elsewhere and in directions where his great armies might march unimpeded to accomplish victories crafted by his undeniable military genius.

On the 20th of November, 1805, a combined allied force of Russian and British troops, under the command of General Sir James Craig, landed at Naples to contribute to the defence of this small Italian kingdom positioned usefully on the shores of the middle sea. The Neapolitan, King Ferdinand (who was also King of Sicily), had decided to ally himself, principally with Austria, though in consequence with the alliance of nation states which formed the Third Coalition opposing Napoleon's France. These states included the Holy Roman Empire, Russia, Britain, Sweden and the union Kingdom of Sicily. The diminutive Kingdom of Naples was incapable of making a significant contribution to the greater war effort, so its own future security was in peril in the absence of support by foreign troops.

The Treaty of Amiens between Britain and France, signed in March 1802 as a 'definitive treaty of peace, friendship and understanding' had endured for just thirteen months, only to be

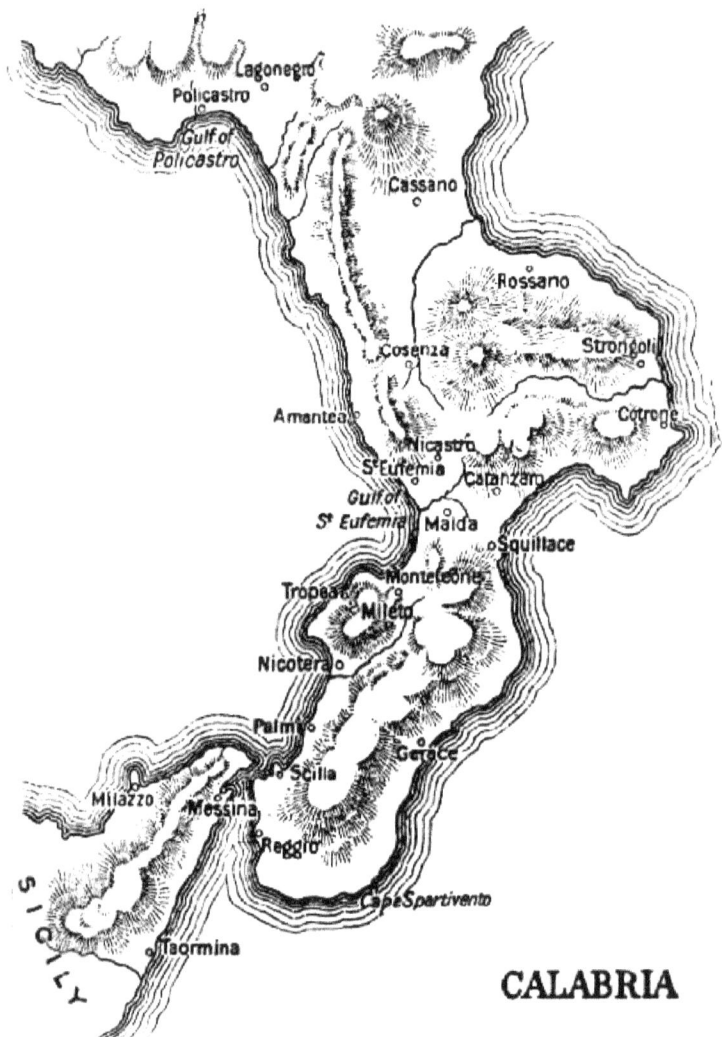

CALABRIA

terminated by Britain with a declaration of war, since it could no longer disregard Napoleon's flagrant advances in Switzerland, Germany, the Netherlands and Italy. Whilst the Royal Navy had ensured that the armies of France would turn away from the continental shore of the English Channel, British good fortune meant ill fortune at the hands of Napoleon would befall someone before much time had elapsed and so it was that the road from Boulogne led to Austerlitz. That battle, which inflicted a severe defeat upon the Austrians and Russians on the 2nd of December, 1805, shook continental Europe to the core, for it seemed that Napoleon was possessed of an insuperable will and ability to conquer whomever and wherever he chose to deploy his armies.

Napoleon was perpetually aware of the ideal times to play his advantages and that there was never a better time than immediately following the delivery of a severe military object lesson. Furthermore, never one to be influenced by a deterrent he had calculated had neither the resources or determination to abide by its intentions, he unilaterally declared, on the 27th of December, 1805, that 'the dynasty of Naples had ceased to reign.' The French Army marched to take possession of Naples and Napoleon's unexceptional older brother, Joseph, implausibly re-profiled as Giuseppe I, was nominated to place his accommodating bottom on the Neapolitan throne.

Having seen both the mighty Holy Roman Empire and Russia humbled, the Neapolitan royal family could think of nothing but that they had backed the wrong side and, indeed, that view was at the time understandable for the defeat at Austerlitz effectively put an end to the Third Coalition of allies that had opposed the French. Perhaps, more in hope than any expectation of reprieve, King Ferdinand and his queen, Maria Carolina of Austria (sister of the executed Marie Antoinette), pleaded with Napoleon for forgiveness, but their entreaties predictably availed them nothing. The Neapolitan king's discomfort was exacerbated by the fact that he had previously entered into a treaty with Napoleon concerning southern Italy, upon which he had demonstrably reneged. The emperor was reliably never one to pass by the opportunities presented by an excellent pretext.

In January, 1806 without disputing the matter with the usurpers by force of arms, the Neapolitan court quit mainland Italy and fled (or retreated, dependent on perspective) to Sicily accompanied by the British contingent, while the Russian troops who had formed a portion of the foreign Neapolitan defence force, embarked for Corfu in the Ionian Islands. Joseph Bonaparte entered Naples as sovereign on the 15th of the following month. The forces of the Kingdoms of Naples and Sicily subsequently offered resistance, but were defeated at Campo Tenese in early March.

In the spring of the year 1806, Sir James Craig resigned the command of the British Army on Sicily and the defence of the island was transferred to the command of Sir John Stuart. Given the less than advantageous circumstances which had placed his force on an island in the Mediterranean in close proximity to the enemy, it was obvious to Stuart that the French would not long tolerate his position and that he could, in all likelihood, expect a French invasion of Sicily, for the narrow Strait of Messina, between the toe of the Italian boot and the island, was no English Channel.

Stuart concluded that his best option was a pre-emptive offensive which, if it was successful, would fulfil three objectives. Firstly, he might 'wrong foot' the French before they launched their own attack, thereby destroying some of their preparations whilst giving the enemy sobering notice of what they could expect from an engagement with a British Army. Secondly, a decisive strike would inspire and inflame the spirit of insurrection which yet burned among the people of Calabria, and finally a demonstration of the will to take the fight to the enemy might encourage the besieged coastal garrison of Gaeta, though it remained defiant in a position of undeniable isolation, far from his own comparatively small force and some distance north of Naples itself. The hoped-for relief of the Gaeta garrison by Stuart (which in any event was not his brief) was problematic to the point of unlikely.

Setting sail with an army of British regulars with artillery and supported by Swiss, Corsican and Sicilian troops, Stuart crossed over to Italy, on the 1st of July with about 5,000 men who came ashore, landing without resistance on the Gulf of St. Euphemia (Golfo de Santa Euphemia) approximately 100 miles north of the northern coast of Sicily. The enemy was already close at hand near the town of Maida under the command of General Jean Reynier, with in the region of 5,500-6,000 French troops, which constituted the bulk of the enemy in that part of Calabria, under his command.

Though the details of the Battle of Maida fought on the 4th of July are interesting, they are not pertinent to the principal narrative of this book. Suffice it to note that the engagement was a short and decisive British victory which some commentators have gone so far as to term a 'drubbing', since allied casualties amounted to 327 and those of the enemy were in excess of 2,000. Stuart mopped up pockets of French troops positioned in garrisons south of the battlefield towards his Sicilian base, but these actions could not assist the isolated besieged Neapolitans of the Gaeta garrison, which was forced to capitulate to Masséna on the 18th of July, releasing up to12,000 more French troops for duty elsewhere.

Stuart established himself for a time at Silla (Scylla) at the mouth of the Gulf of Messina on the Italian mainland, but towards the end of the year withdrew his forces once again to Sicily. He was shortly afterwards transferred to Malta, and was succeeded in Sicily by General Henry Fox, an obese man in clearly poor health who, in fact, died in 1811 aged just 56 years. However, during his time in Sicily his incapacities meant that placed reliance on his able second in command, Sir John Moore, who would shortly make a notable appearance in the conflict which would soon erupt on the Iberian Peninsula.

Some months before this change of generals, the British Government had already determined to substantially reinforce the army in the Mediterranean, and to put into action initiatives intended to prevent Napoleon from taking possession of Sicily.

The Battle of Maida

CHAPTER THREE

The First Guards on Sicily

In 1806, two battalions of the First Guards, the first and the third, under Colonel F. G. Lake and Colonel Moore Disney, which formed the First Brigade of Guards under General Wynyard, were in their barracks at Chatham on the Medway. The area contained valuable naval dockyards (Nelson's flag ship '*Victory*' had been launched there) and extensive defensive works to protect them from potential continental raids or invasions; considered a very real threat as the Dutch raid on the Medway of the later 17th century had demonstrated.

Orders were received by the Guards in early July, at about the time Stuart and his force were crossing over to Italy to fight at Maida, to ensure that there were 120 able bodied men available per company and to prepare for immediate foreign service. A fortnight later, on the 26th of July, the brigade set out upon its 40-mile march to the port at Ramsgate, whereupon arrival both the first battalion and the third battalion embarked on board their transport ships.

Also, on board this fleet anchored in the Downs was a brigade of the infantry of the line. Bad weather delayed sailing on two occasions until the ships at last set sail in mid-August, coasting down the English Channel to anchor in Plymouth Sound, where another brigade of line infantry supported by cavalry boarded. All seemed finally ready to leave for the southward voyage, when naval priorities necessitated an immediate disembarkation of the army and in the first days of September, after a month of delays, the Guards marched to Bickleigh Down, some 5 or 6 miles from Plymouth, where they went into camp. In the meantime, six flank companies of the two Guards battalions had been formed into a separate unit. Among the officers of the Third Battalion, First Guards embarking on this expedition was Lieutenant-Captain, Lord Saltoun, then in his twenty first year.

In the prestigious Guards, officers held two ranks—a regimental one which was lower than their army rank, since the former was required to correspond with the command structure of a regimental unit. This peculiar arrangement meant that, at this time, the regimental majors and the senior captains were all major-generals in the army, whilst two others were brigadier-generals and all these officers, by virtue of high rank, returned to staff duties.

Accordingly, the Guards reinforcements bound for Sicily were constituted as follows: The flank battalion of 725 men was commanded by Clinton. The first battalion of 919 men was commanded by Lake. And the third battalion of 915 men was under Moore Disney. The total strength of the brigade was 2,559 men under the command of Wynyard.

The brigade embarked once again in mid-September, under the protection of the Royal Navy's 100-gun war ship, *Royal George*. The fleet then set sail, though it was not until late October, in consequence of perpetual bad weather, that it anchored in the Bay of Tangiers, arriving in Tetuan Bay on the first day of November.

Among the transports carrying part of the light infantry battalion of the First Guards, was a collier brig, *Christopher*, which lost her foremast during a gale in the Bay of Biscay and becoming separated from the convoy, then lost her way. The ship's captain sailed for three weeks by his own reckoning, but had no idea where he was. One evening as night drew in, Sergeant-Major Colquhoun noticed the sea had much changed colour, which he knew was an indication that the vessel was close to land. Colquhoun passed on his observations to his commanding officer who in turn spoke to the vessel's captain.

The *Royal George*, (right) at Chatham

The sailor laughed, declaring they were more than 100 miles from any coast. However, on gauging his depth he discovered, to his surprise, no more than ten fathoms under the keel and, as the light improved the following morning, nearby land appeared. The transport was anchored, and the Guards, as a precaution, were served with ammunition. Before long, boats were sighted setting out from the shore and their occupants brought news that they were off the mouth of the Spanish river, Guadalquivir, north of Cadiz, close under the guns of the batteries of Rota. *Christopher* was towed further out to sea during the night and put in charge of a brig-of-war, which guided them safely to Gibraltar. The progress of the main fleet, though unimpeded by misadventures, had been painfully slow and it was not until December that the Guards finally entered the Bay of Messina, nearly three months after they had left England.

In later life, Saltoun wrote to his friend 'Charley' Ellis, who joined the First Guards in 1811 as an ensign and became, in due course, Saltoun's subaltern. He was still by Saltoun's side four years later at Waterloo and was wounded during the action at Hougoumont.

> We reached Sicily about the middle of December 1806, having coasted along the whole island, from the little island of Marstino to the town of Messina at the head of the strait of that name, having sailed along a most beautiful mountainous country, in many places, particularly near Messina, studded with villas, having Etna in view the whole time; and one of the finest sights was to see the sun strike the top of Etna on rising, which it did about five minutes before you saw it, and lit the mountains down by degrees till you were aware that the sun was up, also the snow on the top, when first struck by the sun, looking like an immense ball of fire.

Instead of landing immediately, the transports carrying the brigade were ordered to Catania, some miles to the south on the island's eastern coast and to disembark their men there. The First Guards, including the flank companies, disembarked on the 6th of December at the port of Catania, which sits at the foot

Lipari

Vulcano

Cape Faro

Scylla

Milazzo

MESSINA

Reggio

CALABRIA

C. Calava

Flank
Battalion
in 1806

Contessa
Light
Companies
in 1807

Millia

C. Orlando

Patti

Melita

Pellaro

STRAITS OF MESSINA

2nd Comp.
Battn.

Posts along the Coast

Taormina

MESSINA

Ali

Aci

Posts along the Coast

3rd Battn.
2 Comp.

1st Battn.
6 Comp.

CATANIA
Head Quarters
GEN. WYNYARD

LAKE

R. Garita

Plain
of
Catania

Paulo

Dittano

MEDITERRANEAN SEA

Augusta

Meca R.

EXPEDITION

TO

SICILY

AND OCCUPATION OF

EAST COAST

BY

FIRST GUARDS

1806 & 1807.

1807
Flank Battn.
2 Comp.

CLINTON

SYRACUSE

Noto

R. Abysso

R. Butalem

Scale of Eng. miles
5 0 5 10 15 20

C. Passaro

of the volcano of Mount Etna. Once ashore six companies of the third battalion, under Colonel Disney, were temporarily sent 40 miles farther down the coast to the ancient city of Syracuse. Troops moved occasionally to different locations, but essentially the battalions of the First Guards were distributed in the principal posts along the east coast of Sicily, extending from Messina to Syracuse, for about eighty or ninety miles.

Major-General Wynyard placed his headquarters at Catania which enabled him to readily command the district. General Fox, as Commander-in-Chief, resided at Messina with Captain John Colborne as his military secretary. Colborne, a soldier of whom it was said, 'had a singular talent for war', was destined to become a notable figure in the Peninsular War and upon the field of Waterloo where, in command of the 52nd· as part of Adams' Brigade, he would deliver the *coup de grace* to the flanks of advancing columns of Napoleon's Imperial Guard at the close of the battle

Despite their role as protectors of the island and its royal family, the British troops were viewed by the population at large as unwelcome interlopers and were generally unpopular. At the beginning of the year 1807, the British forces on the island, including Wynyard's brigade of Guards, amounted to 18,000 men, and there were also about 14,000 Neapolitan troops available for deployment in the event of an attack.

In northern Europe, Napoleon's campaigns brought about political consequences which were the British Government's principal concerns. Defeats of the previous year had overturned the Prussian monarchy and the disheartened Russians had retired to the Niemen, but the *Tsar* had refused to ratify a peace and rumours spoke of some Russian successes in Poland. Ready to grasp at any straw which might make the restoration of the Neapolitan throne more probable, the exiled queen lobbied for an attack upon Naples to be undertaken with the support of the British Army at hand. General Fox, however, had no confidence in the prospects of this initiative and though resolved to keep a firm hold on Sicily, would not risk the army operating farther afield.

In the spring of 1807, the British Government removed the option of an expedition onto the Italian mainland by seconding 5,000 men of the regiments of the line stationed in Sicily for an ill-fated expedition to Alexandria, while at the same time it sent a fleet to the Dardanelles in an attempt to dissuade the Turks from going to war against Russia at Napoleon's behest. Desperation drove the Neapolitan queen, despite the hopelessness of the enterprise, to launch an unsupported invasion of Calabria, but her troops were inevitably defeated by the French in late May. The much-depleted ranks of the expedition to Alexandria returned to Sicily in October.

Although there was no actual fighting for the Guards stationed on Sicily, the fact the enemy lay perilously close across the narrow Strait of Messina, meant a strict watch had to be kept upon French movements to be in readiness to meet any hostile attempt to cross over to the island.

Lord Saltoun was involved in an incident at this time, the details of which were recorded in a memorandum, and which, to use his own words, showed 'how little attention your English soldier pays to anything, unless long service and severe experience has driven something like observation into him.' This incident is interesting in its own right and though Saltoun describes his own part in these events in a matter of fact manner, his narrative, all be it unintentionally, gives the reader an insight into this very young officer's physical strength and determination, especially bearing in mind the fates of others who were involved.

We had been some months at Contessa, when the French, who since the Battle of Maida had remained in upper Calabria, suddenly marched a large force down to the straits of Messina, commenced a sort of siege of the Castle of Scilla, where we had a garrison, and taking possession of Regio, a town on the coast, nearly opposite our cantonments, began collecting boats and making preparations to invade Sicily. A party of an officer and 30 men was established at a place called Milia, about six miles from our cantonments, in order to give the alarm should any landing take place about there; and we communicated by small posts of a corporal and three men at certain distances all along

20th Light Dragoons, Sicily, 1806–7

the line, to a particular point from which it was about 3 miles to Milia, which post was visited every night by the captain on duty, and a patrol of a corporal and file of dragoons went from Messina to Milia twice during the night.

It had rained most of the evening, and I had started a little later than usual to go my rounds, and I had met the first patrol on its return from Milia, a little before I came to the great *fiumara* or watercourse, which ran from the mountains into the strait; in summer this was in general dry, or at most very small, but in heavy rains often impassable, and on the Milia side of this *fiumara* was situated our extreme corporal's picquet on the right, our left one communicating with the Citadel of Messina.

When I crossed the *fiumara* it was running a strong stream, but nothing dangerous. I proceeded on to Milia and visited the post there, stayed a short time, and smoked a cigar with the officer. According to the time of the patrol, I ought to have met it between the *fiumara* and Milia, but I did not, and when I came to the *fiumara* I at once saw that it was utterly impassable; it was raging with a force that would have carried away an elephant, and in the current of the burn, from the stones it covered at the sides, must have been more than ten feet deep. I made no doubt but that the patrol finding it in this state had returned.

This ford was about 200 yards above the junction of the *fiumara* with the sea, which is so deep, close to land all along that part of the straits of Messina, that a man-of-war could tack with its bowsprit over the land.

As I had no inclination to stay there in the rain I coasted the torrent down to its junction with the sea, and being an excellent swimmer myself, as well as in the constant habit at that time of swimming my horse, I at once put him into the deep water, and without any difficulty reached the other side, and proceeded on my rounds. I found that the patrol had visited all the posts on its way out as usual, and on reaching the cavalry post at Messina, as I was obliged to mention in my report the circumstance of my not having met the patrol, I inquired of the officer about it, and found that it had not returned.

I mentioned my fears for it to the officer, but as it was possible that they had taken some shelter to wait till the *fiumara* should run off, a sergeant was sent to look for them and bring them back, but they were never heard of afterwards, and as desertion was impracticable, at least with their horses, and moreover a crime not at all prevailing in the English part of the army at that time, there can be no doubt but they were carried away in trying to ford the *fiumara*.

During their comparatively uneventful stay in Sicily, the officers who could procure leave, assembled shooting parties and a pack of hounds also enabled them to engage in their favourite pastime. Exploring expeditions took place all over the island, visiting the ancient temples, Girgente, and others, describing them in 'a true antiquarian spirit'. The young Saltoun was no exception to the rule and in his letters large sections are dedicated to descriptions of the ancient ruins of Sicily which, since they bear little on the focus of this account, have been excised from this edition.

Saltoun's letter to his mother, Margery, (sometimes spelled Marjory), Fraser, Lady Saltoun, written during this period and a month before his 22nd birthday illustrates that the Sicily Expedition was unlikely to offer the opportunity of active soldiering and we have the impression that he was fairly much a young man at liberty for leisure. Nevertheless, this letter is included at this point, notwithstanding it reads more like a traveller's excursion report than anything other because, devoid of action though it is, it describes from a personal perspective the experience of serving in Sicily for the officers and men of the First Guards in 1807.

18th March 1807.
Catania, Sicily,

Dear Mother,

I wrote you by the last pacquet from Messina, informing you that I was fortunate enough to receive your letters at Palermo, where I was on a tour round the island.

I say fortunate, as most likely I should not have received them for some time, if at all, as Palermo is three days' journey from this place by the nearest road, and the country post so badly regulated that one-half of the letters are lost, and we have no correspondence by means of dragoons with that side of the island, which is entirely under the government of the King; so if you wish me to get any letter punctually, do not send it that way, but if it does not signify how soon I receive it, they may as well go there as anywhere else, as Mr. Drummond will keep them till he has some safe conveyance for them either to this place, or indeed to this side of the island, as there is a regular military post twice a week from Malazzo (*Milazzo*) to Cape Passero.

I have obeyed your instructions in every particular, and sent the letters enclosed in two separate packets, as it was impossible to get them conveyed in one to Messina, where the mail for England is made up. The circular letters I have signed on the inside, but not on the back, as I do not know their separate destinies. The letters to the Dukes of York and Cumberland I have put in a cover and directed; those to the other peers I have directed on the back, and you can put them in covers and send them. They are all open, in order that they may be sealed with my arms. *(Refers to his candidature for election as a Representative Peer.)* Our tour to Palermo was delightful. We had the finest weather possible; the country very beautiful; but as to the accommodation on the road you can have no idea of anything so bad. We were obliged to carry our beds with us, and, as it was *starvation* time, our provisions also; and the inns were so bad that we slept more than once in *lettigas*, (horse-litters for journeys) rather than go into them, notwithstanding which I got my bed so full of fleas and bugs that I was obliged to boil the mattress as the only way of getting them out of it.

Our first day's journey was to Calata Girone, 43 miles. Our way led over the plain of Catania, through Palagonia, a pretty little village. We reached Calata Girone at six at night. It is situated on an immense hill, and is the largest inland town in Sicily, and as dirty. The only thing worth seeing is the view from the top of the great church; and at the Franciscan convent, about half a mile from the town, on the road to Terra Nova, there is a most beautiful figure of a Madonna and child in marble, which is the best bit of sculpture I have yet seen in the island. They do not know who made it, but tell you some cock-and-bull story of the Virgin having made it a present to St. Francis when he was doing Peñance in a wood near the convent.

We left Calata Girone at nine, and after seeing the Madonna, proceeded on to Terra Nova through a most beautiful country, and across the forest of Calata Girone, the second in size in Sicily, I got a shot at a partridge, the only one I had seen in the island, and killed him. He was a very fine bird of the red leg kind, but not half so good eating as our sort of partridge.

We got to Terra Nova at three, probably so called from the flat on which it stands having been gained from the sea, as it has very much that appearance. We found the way very hot, and so went into the sea, which so astonished the natives, that they turned out one and all—men, women, and children—to see us bathe, and could not conceive how we could bathe in the winter, and confessed to us that when it was very cold they did not even wash themselves.

Terra Nova has a small port, at which there is some importation of corn, but very trifling, as the exportation laws of this country are, as far as regards corn, so very nefarious that the farmer cannot afford to send the corn out of the island except at the free ports, for which liberty they pay some tax to the king.

From Terra Nova we went the next day to Alicata, a well-built town and a free port. There is a castle here from which you have a fine sea view—they call it a garrison—which consists of fifty old men who can hardly stand, without arms or ammunition.

The next day we reached Girgenti; on our road there we breakfasted at Palma, a place which Swinbourne mentions as being notorious for rascals, so much so, says he, that not a jail in the country is without more than one Palmanese in it for murder or for theft. The present generation are not far behind them in that science, as they contrived to steal a couple of bottles of wine from us, and our meat-basket; however, we found them out before they could get away, and on producing our pistols they produced the meat.

The approach from Palma to Girgenti is beautiful, through the most fertile country in Sicily, and close by the ruins of the ancient temples. Girgenti, old Agrigentum, is, generally speaking, the best place worth seeing in the world for antiquarians, as the remains of the Greek antiquities are more perfect there than at any other place. However, the temple of all others that one would wish to have seen is that one of Jupiter Olympius, the columns of which were of a most gigantic size, and the fluting of them large enough to contain a man. This temple, I am sorry to say, is no longer in existence; but from what remains, the enormous size of the pillars is clearly to be perceived. Two capitals, which are the only remains of them, are broken in four pieces; and in the small part of the pillar still attached to one of them, Montgomery, who is rather a thin man, could get into the flute with all ease.

In the great church at Girgenti there is a very fine picture of the Virgin and Child by Guido Reni, and also a beautiful antique, a representation of the story of Hippolytus and Phaedra; there is also another singular circumstance, which is, that a person getting up above the altar, can hear anything said at the other end of the church even in a whisper. This is said to have been discovered in the following manner:—A carpenter was up there one day mending the figure of a dragon, and saw his wife come in to confess. He was surprised at so plainly hearing the priest speak to her, and therefore listened and heard the whole of her confession. On returning home he gave her wholesome correction for what he had overheard, and made a regular practice of mending the dragon whenever any rich person went to confess, by which means he got together a good deal of money.

We left Girgenti, and the third day after reached Palermo. The packet has arrived, but I have received neither letters nor papers. I conclude they are to come by Palermo. We are all in perfect health, and some of the men talk of going home to be married, or, in other words, to go out;—the more the better!

With best love to all at home, I am, dear mother, your dutiful son,

Saltoun.

Catania, 2nd April, 1807

In the course of the summer of 1807 the possibility of an invasion of Naples by a combined British and Neapolitan force from Sicily re-emerged as a suggestion from the British Government, though the practicability of this proposal was left to General Fox's judgement. However, irrespective of the general's opinion, the idea was so poorly greeted among the population that the initiative was soon abandoned. It is probable that the Sicilians had little reason to have faith in the success of such an enterprise, based on the outcomes of previous military engagements, believing that 'awakening the sleeping dog' would only bring the weight of the enemy down on the island. Ill feeling ran high and civil disturbances were expected which, were they to escalate, would require already unpopular foreign troops to suppress them, which would have certainly exacerbated antipathy towards the British presence, notwithstanding the support they were providing to the Sicilian Government.

General Fox resigned his post in Sicily in July, 1807, and returned to England whereupon the command devolved upon Sir John Moore. News arrived in August of another French victory in the wider theatre of the war; the defeat of the Russians at Friedland. More than ever, there seemed no impediment to discourage a French Army from marching anywhere it wished in Europe. Moore was left with no illusions as to the tenuous position of his command isolated in Sicily and so began to make preparations for what he believed would be an inevitable and imminent attack from the French on the island. To make matters worse, in the hot weather sickness swept among the troops. Many men were soon in hospital, and still more of them were pronounced unfit for duty. Colonel Salisbury of the First Guards died in the middle of September and was buried in the church of San Filippo.

The First Guards had not much longer to serve on Sicily and the fortunes of the Kingdom of Naples were not destined to soon revive. After Joseph Bonaparte had departed the throne (undergoing another tragicomic change of national identity to become King Jose I of Spain), he was replaced by the flamboyant commander of Napoleon's cavalry, Joachim Murat who had married one of the emperor's sisters, Caroline. His reign of the Kingdom of Naples was destined to end fatally before a firing squad comprised of his less than enamoured 'subjects'. The dispossessed Neapolitan royal family would only regain a measure of its former position after the end of the Napoleonic era in 1815, though the queen by this time had already died in Austria.

CHAPTER FOUR

The Invasion of Portugal, 1807

Since Spain remained a monarchy, the French Revolution was justifiably seen, as it was by all the monarchies of Europe, as a threat of cataclysmic proportions. However, for Spain the situation was particularly acute for the spirit of insurrection was an infection which would take little encouragement to spread across the Pyrenees to pollute an impoverished Iberia. The Spanish monarch had agreed, therefore, to join the First Coalition in an attempt to put an end to the French Republic and restore a Bourbon to the throne of France. Despite encouraging beginnings on land and sea, the French forces proved irresistible and the Peace of Basel in 1795 forced a weakened Spain to quit the coalition. Spanish national status was about enter decades of sharp decline.

The following year brought forth an extraordinary *volte-face* when a Franco-Spanish alliance was formed and Spain found itself at war with Britain as an ally of the new republic. This war, which concluded in 1802, also did not go well for Spain, principally because the Royal Navy succeeded in establishing an economically damaging blockade, though the numerical superiority of the Spanish Mediterranean fleet forced the British from the islands of Corsica and Elba. The Treaty of Amiens provided a short lull in hostilities, but when the British reacted to French provocations, the Royal Navy came back into action and in 1804 attacked and captured most of a treasure fleet of Spanish frigates.

As has been explained, this was the time of Napoleon's proposed invasion of Britain, the success of which required a period of naval superiority and the participation of the Spanish navy was an essential element in the acquiring of an advantage at sea. Nelson, by defeating the Franco-Spanish fleet at Trafalgar, not only put an end to that scheme forever, but arguably provoked the catalyst by which Napoleon ceased to see Spain as a useful, if temporary, ally. The emperor, with his insatiable desire for conquest, determined to subjugate the whole Iberian Peninsula and he built his gambit, as he had done so often, upon the foundations of a grand deceit.

Following the Battle of Friedland, Napoleon had signed an armistice with the Emperor of Russia, which resulted in the signing of the Treaty of Tilsit (7th of July, 1807). This treaty required Russia, among others, to adhere to the emperor's ruling of the 'Continental System,' which was intended to ruin the commercial capabilities of Great Britain by excluding her ships from all the ports of Europe. The Portuguese at first acceded to the emperor's demands, but when the British responded by sending a fleet to blockade the Tagus, reversed that policy, refusing after motivated reconsideration, to take exclusive measures against their ally.

Napoleon could not allow such a defiance to go unpunished and proposed a treaty, couched in terms which promised many attractive material gains for Spain, by which it was agreed that the combined armies of the two nations should over-run and divide Portugal between them. A substantial French Army was assembled at Bayonne, and, in 1807, Napoleon decreed, in his typical imperious fashion, that 'the reigning House of Braganza had ceased to exist in Portugal'. General Junot at the head of 'The First Corps of Observation of the Gironde' comprising some 25,000 men, was then directed to march towards Lisbon; a route, that hardly requires emphasis, which which would necessitate large numbers of French troops on Spanish soil initially, and given success, indefinitely.

Orders arrived in Sicily early in October, 1807, directing Sir

John Moore to immediately embark 7,600 men of his army to Gibraltar, where he would receive further directions as to their ultimate destination. Among their number was the Brigade of First Guards, together with other regiments of the line. Moore boarded the *Queen*, a 98-gun three-tiered ship of the line, and the fleet sailed for Gibraltar at the end of the month, leaving Sir John Sherbrook with 6,000 men to protect Sicily. The unpredictability of sail once again influenced the journey, so the fleet did not arrive at its destination until the first day of December. Moore here discovered the disheartening news that the frigate, *Volage* had carried out a dispatch for him, whilst he had been *en route,* ordering him not to leave Sicily. Colonel Disney's appointment as brigadier-general was also confirmed, with orders that he should return to Sicily.

Sir John Moore now learned the details of his original orders which were that he should proceed to Lisbon, where he was to have been joined by 8,000 men under the experienced General Brent Spencer, to support the king and the Prince Regent of Portugal. By this point, however, the time for intercession was past, for the French had almost arrived in Lisbon and the Portuguese royal family, believing it impossible to resist them, had already quit the capital with the rest of their supporters, and had set sail for South America. General Junot's force, in consequence, marched into Lisbon without opposition. For Napoleon there was nothing discouraging about the outcome of his stratagems which appeared, at the time, to be not only to be not only well founded as to their immediate outcomes, but also particularly promising for further easily achieved objectives in the Iberian Peninsula.

Moore, nevertheless, considered it was worthwhile to personally go to Lisbon, since a Royal Navy presence under Sir Sydney Smith lay off-shore, to determine whether a landing would be of any advantage, but discovered upon his arrival there that any intervention by him would be futile. He therefore returned to Gibraltar, and leaving two line regiments on the rock, set sail again for England in mid-December with the Guards and remainder of his troops.

In a letter to a fellow officer, Saltoun wrote a slightly different perspective of the confused state of affairs at this time.

> We left Sicily in the autumn of 1807, forming part of a force of 10,000 men, with Sir John Moore. Our first instructions were to take Ceuta, (on the North African coast.) but they thought it too strong. We were then (in the event of the King of Portugal submitting to the French) to have gone to the Brazils, and taken that; but as the King of Portugal abandoned his kingdom, and went to the Brazils himself, Sir John Moore brought us to England.

The first and third battalions, First Guards landed at Portsmouth and marched to their barracks, arriving in the first days of 1808. In consequence of his promotion to lieutenant-general, in May, 1808, General Wynyard, the second major of the regiment, who had commanded the First Brigade for five years departed. Major-General Warde, the senior captain and lieutenant-colonel, succeeded him and Major-General Henry Campbell was appointed to command the Second Brigade of Guards until the return of Major-General Moore Disney from Sicily.

Saltoun took the opportunity offered by this hiatus to visit his family. His widowed mother was living at this time in Dartmouth House, Blackheath, south of the River Thames in order to be near her father. In fact, Saltoun's earlier years had been spent in England, and it is doubtful whether he had ever, since his succession to the title, visited his paternal estates. So, in the autumn he travelled northward to Philorth and Fraserburgh and thereafter took a tour of Scotland to visit relatives and friends.

CHAPTER FIVE

The Peninsular Campaign of 1808

In late November of 1807, the French 'Second Corps of Observation of the Gironde' under Dupont and some 30,000 men strong began to filter into northern Spain ostensibly *en route* for Portugal, whilst making little discernible progress in that direction. Several more 'corps of observation' followed, crossing the Franco-Spanish border and spreading out over the country, securing vital positions as they went. By the time 'The Army of Observation of the Eastern Pyrenees', under Duheseme had moved into Catalonia on the Mediterranean coast in the middle of February it was obvious to all that these armies had not come to 'observe' and were definitely not going to Portugal.

A rift in the Spanish royal family between Charles IV and his son, Ferdinand, exacerbated by the politicking of First Secretary, Manuel Godoy brought matters to a head. Napoleon removed the troublesome and weak Spanish royal family having lured them into France. Joseph Bonaparte's obliging posterior once again became useful and his brother placed it on the throne of Spain. Madrid was quickly taken, but the populace rose up in aggrieved indignation and slaughtered numbers of their occupiers which provoked a brutal reprisal by the French. Though Napoleon did not understand it at the time, for he was ignorant of the Spanish character, this was the first indication that he had 'grasped the tiger by the tail'.

The Spanish people maintained a jaundiced view of their aristocracy and had little faith in their politicians or military com-

BLACKHEATH, WITH A VIEW TOWARDS LONDON, EARLY 19TH CENTURY

PHILORTH HOUSE, EARLY 19TH CENTURY

manders. Indeed, Spanish military resources were very low and the poorly organised Spanish troops were incapable of offering more than feeble resistance to the veterans of France. However, they were certain of their identity as Spaniards and that the country they knew to be their own was invaded by a foreign army which could never be tolerated or allowed to abide. This will to endure in spite of any defeats or consequences is in itself a most powerful opponent and one impossible to master.

The flame of patriotism and resistance, within armies, guerillas and peasants alike, was kindled throughout the land and grew into a conflagration of passion which, despite many reverses, refused to be extinguished. Genuine hatred escalated the number and degree of atrocities on both sides until their horrors became emblematic of the entire conflict. Napoleon had inadvertently created the 'Spanish Ulcer', a 'war to the knife' that would fatally drain his resources more than any of his wars.

Nevertheless, by the close of May 1808, the French emperor had marched in excess of 100,000 troops into Spain. The Spanish Supreme Junta, in June 1808, realising the nation's peril, appealed to Britain for succour. The British Government, applying the principle of, 'my enemy's enemy is my friend', put aside past antipathies, ratified a peace with Spain in London on the 6th of July and the two nations became allies. But that this alliance would prove to be as straightforward in practice as it was in its creation.

The French and Spanish continued to fight localised campaigns and battles, but the campaign that primarily concerns this narrative was that undertaken by Junot who, with a force of 28,000 men in Portugal, was holding down the centre of the country and sending out flying columns in the month of June to suppress the uprisings that had flared up all about him.

It is worth noting that Spain soon gave Napoleon further notice that it was not prepared to be submissive, for at the Battle of Baylen fought on July 19th, 1808, its army beat a French Army, which threw Joseph into a panic.

The days of the stalwart Spanish *tercios* were long past, so had the emperor been asked to nominate a candidate who would deliver the first open-field defeat upon his armies in any of his conflicts, he would probably not have chosen a Spanish Army for the laurels. As it transpired, this victory came about less as a result of Spanish military acumen than by the incompetence of the French commander, General Dupont. The details of that battle are less germane to this narrative than that the news of it swept through a cowed Europe and rekindled hope in the hearts of nations which previously could see no future that did not include a virtually omnipotent Napoleon. That inspiration contributed, in due course and among other factors, to persuade the emperor to turn away from a retreating British Army in Spain when it was almost within his grasp.

On the 12th of July, an army (which included no Guards battalions) of about 10,000 men, under the command of Sir Arthur Wellesley, set sail from England, landing on the Portuguese coast at Mondego Bay in the first days of August. Wellesley already had something of a reputation as a '*Sepoy* General', following his victories in India. Indeed, it was his own understanding that he would command the expedition to Portugal, but his family had enemies in the government and so, unknown to him since he had already embarked, he would be at the point they arrived in the field, subordinate to two senior officers. These were Sir Hew Dalrymple, Governor of Gibraltar and Sir Harry Burrard who formerly commanded the First Brigade of Guards, and was still the lieutenant-colonel of the First Guards.

Readers will recall Burrard during the Expedition to the Helder. Though he had done well in defence of Pettin, neither he or Dalrymple were noted as commanders of larger forces or had particularly notable battlefield accomplishments to their credit, particularly compared to Wellesley. However, though few fully appreciated it at this time, Sir Arthur Wellesley's abilities as a commander would set a bar impossibly high for any British general of his day (and few, if any, generals of other nations), for he would become, in due course, the Duke of Wellington and Napoleon's nemesis.

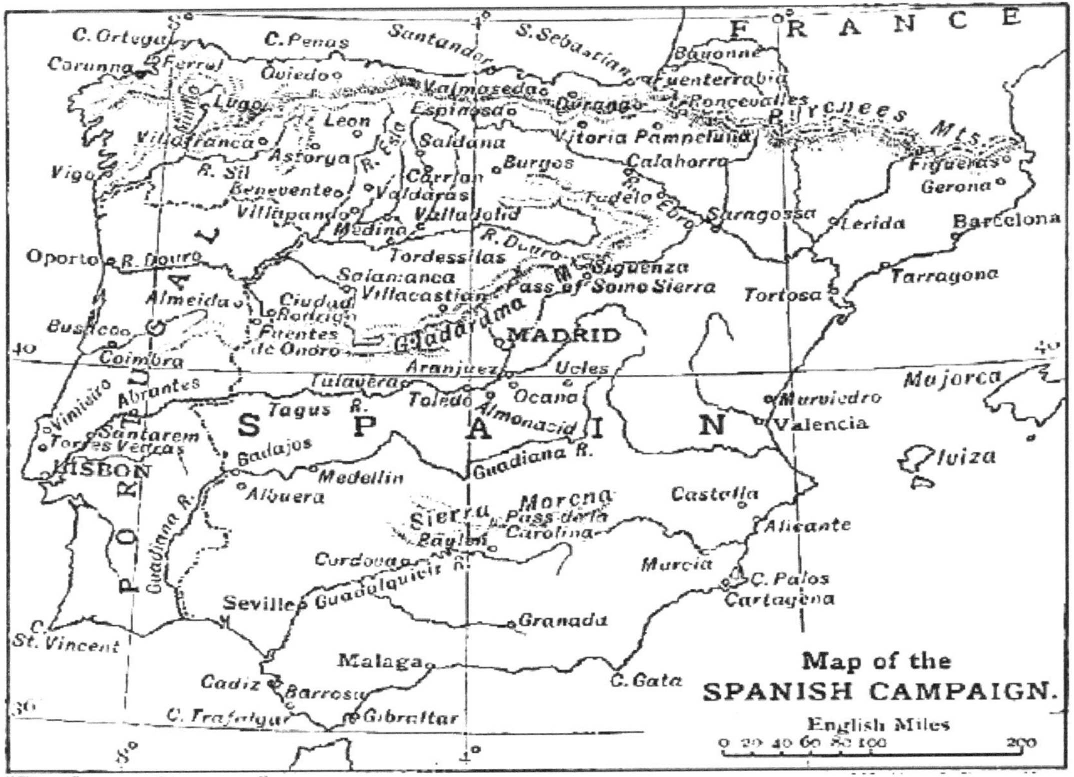

Map of the SPANISH CAMPAIGN.

The plan of the British Government was first to drive the French out of Portugal, and then advance into Spain to co-operate with Spanish armies. On the 17th of August, Wellesley, whose command was now in the region of 13,000 men having been reinforced from home, attacked and drove the French force, under Laborde, which had been despatched by Junot to delay him, from a strong defensive position at Roliça. This was a small but promising beginning, for from lamentations of despair, the cry of victory was for the first time raised in Portugal.

Upon hearing the news of this reverse, Junot came north from Lisbon with 13,000 men to meet the invasion. Wellesley had by now been reinforced by two additional brigades from England, under Brigadier-Generals Anstruther and Ackland, increasing his own force to over 16,000 augmented by the support of 2,500 men from Portuguese regiments and insurgents, including 41 members of the Lisbon Police Cavalry. On the 21st of August, Junot came across the British Army encamped at Vimeiro with its back to the sea and immediately launched an aggressive and impetuous attack against a position which was well placed on a line of rolling hills.

Simply put, this battle would be an early lesson, taught by the master, of the maintenance of a well-situated defensive position with the ideal troops for the purpose and Junot's poorly coordinated assault columns were promptly thrown back with severe losses inflicted by the volleys of the British line. Years hence, Wellington would comment of Waterloo, 'They came on in the same old way and we saw them off in the same old way'. It is tempting to imagine he was tacitly praising the prowess of British soldiers, though justifiably, he was as likely to be speaking quite literally.

At the moment, as Wellesley was about to unleash his reserves to follow up his advantage, matters in Portugal turned sour. Sir Harry Burrard arrived upon the field and stopped the pursuit, apparently for the purpose of waiting for the large reinforcements expected with Sir John Moore who had also been called to the theatre and would, therefore, upon his arrival also be superior to Wellesley. The following day, Sir Hew Dalrymple arrived from Gibraltar and as senior officer assumed overall command of the army. Any impetus that had been created in this campaign now ground to a halt.

Wellesley was, predictably, for marching on Lisbon, inflicting a trouncing and exacting an unconditional surrender from the enemy. Junot, quickly acknowledging that he was about to be beaten, sued for an armistice and proposed a treaty; the infamous Convention of Cintra, which stipulated that the French army of 25,000 men would evacuate Portugal to be transported unmolested by the British back to France together with all the spoils they had plundered during their stay in the country as invaders. Sir Hew Dalrymple agreed to this ostensibly outrageous proposal; a decision which elicited gasps of astonishment and indignation in the British Government and throughout the home country.

Dalrymple's pragmatic arrangement meant, emotive sentiments aside, Portugal had been won cheaply and quickly (so far as the British were concerned) given that time was of the essence and that the policy objective was to liberate Spain. However, seen in the best light, his was a 'statesman's victory' providing meagre satisfaction in the wake of the unambiguous soldier's victory of Vimeiro. Moore, by contrast, had no time for Dalrymple's resolution, abilities or intelligence, so it is possible that this outcome came about more by accident than design. Certainly, many people believed the French had got off unnecessarily lightly and there were numerous complaints from serving officers and from the Portuguese provisional government which would have preferred to see a good deal more French blood spread on the ground.

Dalrymple, Burrard and Wellesley were recalled to England and sent before a court of enquiry which concluded that none of them were to blame for any wrong doing, 'acting to the best of their judgement and with the proper zeal' and so all three of them had the satisfaction of being exonerated. For Dalrymple and Burrard this vindication of their actions meant, in practice, that they were never again sent on active service, whereas Wellesley was returned to Portugal the following Spring as commander-in-chief. In the meantime, the army in Portugal came under the command of Sir John Moore.

Chapter Six

The Brigade of Guards in Spain, 1808

Early in August, as Sir John Moore's command advanced from Lisbon towards central Spain, the British Government decided to send out a further reinforcement of 10,000 men, including a Brigade of Guards, to operate in the north of Spain within a British Army of in the region of 30,000 infantry and 5,000 cavalry. This army would include the first and third battalions (in which Lord Saltoun served with the light company) of the First Guards, commanded respectively by Lieutenant-Colonels Cocks and Wheatley, which formed the First Brigade under Major-General Warde.

These battalions had been quartered at Deal, on the English coast between the North Sea and the English Channel since their return from Sicily and they now marched some twelve miles to Ramsgate and embarked on the 8th of September. The first battalion amounted to 1,511 men of all ranks and the third battalion stood at 1,243 men. Following embarkation, they sailed for the general rendezvous at Falmouth, dropping anchor on the 22nd of September.

The assembled troops, numbering 13,000, under the command of Sir David Baird, were now organised into four brigades. These were the first and third battalions, First Guards under Warde, the 1st, 26th, 27th, and 31st regiments of Foot under Manningham, the 51st, 59th, 60th, 76th and 81st regiments under Mackenzie and Craufurd's 14th, 23rd, 43rd regiments and the second battalion of the Rifles—the 95th. The fleet sailed on the 8th of October, anchoring off Corunna, at the north-western tip of Spain on the 13th of the same month.

Early in October the main body of the army under Sir John Moore had advanced from Lisbon in Portugal and, as if in a portent of things to come, its affairs had gone awry almost immediately. Moore had acted upon what proved to be very bad advice concerning the difficulty of the terrain the army would traverse. This led him to split his force, sending the cavalry and artillery on an unnecessarily circuitous route, on the understanding that the direct way would be problematic for them. Meanwhile, he marched his 16,000 infantry over the mountains, with no apparent difficulty, *via* the fortified town of Almeida on the border with Spain, to Ciudad Rodrigo, where he made his headquarters for a short period, before reaching Salamanca in mid-November. This inauspicious start meant his full force did not come together until early December. Simply put, Moore was in unfamiliar territory, both literally and figuratively, and, it might be fairly suggested that he remained so until his last day.

Moore's first objective had been to join forces with and so offer assistance and cooperation to Spanish armies, but he found them to be disorganised and depleted, for they had paid dearly whenever they engaged the enemy in battle. In the course of the autumn the Spanish Army of the north, under Blake, had been defeated at Espinosa. Another large force had been dispersed by Soult near Burgos and the Spanish generals, Palafox and Castanos, were routed at Tudela.

By early December, Napoleon was in the capital, Madrid having comprehensively thrashed Spanish armies on his way in several battles, for he had realised that to bring about the desired outcome in Spain he could not depend on the talents of his brother, Joseph and that his own intercession was required. To ensure his objectives might be achieved in a timely fashion the emperor had, by this time, little fewer than 300,000 men at his disposal within Spanish borders.

Moore was not long in understanding that any expectation of concerted military operations with the Spaniards was hopeless for several reasons, including a seemingly natural inclination to be uncooperative with their British ally, their perpetual organisational disarray and the fact that their armies were beaten and in retreat. Furthermore, since the French in Spain were now in overwhelming numbers, the position of his own unsupported small army was becoming increasingly more tenuous.

In the meantime, the regional *Junta* of Corunna had astonishingly refused to allow Sir David Baird's division, which had arrived there (as indicated) on the 13th of October (and included the Guards), to land to aid the war effort without the approval of the Central Junta, and that authority did not arrive for several days. Saltoun wrote a letter to his mother at this time which not only reflects the delay and confusion in which British forces in the peninsula found themselves, but also revealed the lack of information, exacerbated by the rumour mill, which is the perennial lot of the regimental soldier. However, much of what appears in the second paragraph of this letter, given it was written some time before the fact, demonstrated his judgement was remarkably astute.

Corunna, Spain
26th October 1808

Dear Mother,

We have been so bothered with orders, counter orders, and reports, that till this morning nothing certain has been known. The Rifle Corps and the Forty-Third Light Infantry have disembarked this morning, and our brigade begins tomorrow.

We have a march of at least 600 miles before we can reach the enemy, and by all accounts are not likely to be very well off on the way, as the only thing the *Junta* can provide for us is black bread and sour wine, which John *(Bull—presumably, meaning the rank and file,—JHL)* will not relish much; and on our arrival we may expect to be in snow during the greatest part of the time, as our position will be on the left of the Spanish Army, and on the left bank of the Ebro between Bilboa and Pampeluna which is the strongest post the French have at present, and it is whispered is to be the first affair that the British will be employed on. Should we succeed in driving out the enemy, which

THE BRITISH PENINSULAR ARMY IN CAMP

is not so easily done as you have settled it in the city, I dare say we shall proceed to Italy, which will be rather better than Spain. There are at present no less than eight people packing up in the cabin, and the noise they make is such that no person can write, or indeed do anything else. I wrote Houston by the last packet, which, as the wind has been fair, he will most likely have received.

Let my letters be sent if possible, in General Warde's First Guards' bag, as by that means I shall get them sooner and more securely. You must not be surprised at hearing seldom, as a sub-altern has not so many opportunities of writing as a general, and our allowance of baggage is so small, that we are obliged to leave even our writing-desks behind us, which is a monstrous inconvenience, but we must put up with it. I am to carry 100 lbs., including bed, etc., which is more than half.

We have no news of any consequence, and the army is tolerably healthy. With best love to all at home,

I am, dear mother, your dutiful son,

Saltoun.

The First Battalion, First Guards disembarked at Corunna two days after the date of Saltoun's letter, and the third battalion disembarked on the following day. A writer of the period noted:

The conduct of the officers and soldiers of the Guards was highly to their credit from the time they disembarked; fewer excesses were committed by those men than many regiments of similar numbers, and their officers preferred sharing with them their quarters, to profiting by the billets offered them. Out of 2,500 men, when they were put in motion, they only left 20 sick at Corunna: other regiments not half their number left twice as many.

Moore meanwhile, despite his forebodings and the realisation that his was an isolated independent command with approaching 300 miles dividing him from Baird, resolved to be of assistance to the conflict with the resources he already had at his disposal. To that end, he decided to hinder the French armies advance into the south of the country by throwing himself on their lines of communication. This diversion was so successful that the French corps *en route* for Valencia, Badajoz, and Saragossa were halted and Napoleon put aside all other considerations so that he could draw upon whatever resources he decided were necessary to crush the British Army in Spain.

In the north of the country Baird's division at last left Corunna. The Brigade of Guards marched to Santiago, arriving in the first days of November. It then marched by wings to Lugo, and after halting two days advanced to Cambanos in the vicinity of Astorga, Leon on the 23rd and 24th of November. Baird then divided his force into two divisions, one of which was placed under Major-General Warde, whereupon the command of the Brigade of First Guards temporarily devolved to Colonel William Anson, one of the acting majors; the flank companies being formed into a battalion under Colonel John Lambert.

Whilst at Astorga, Baird learned that the enemy was in force at Rio Seco, so he halted to concentrate his troops, but then received orders from Sir John Moore that he should, though it was barely a month after he had landed, fall back on Corunna, embark again and sail to Lisbon. The First Guards retired on the last days of November, moving towards Villafranca and Nogales; the six flank companies, under Colonel Lambert, were detached from the main column on the 1st of December to proceed to Cacabolos, and rejoined it at Herrerias.

Little time had elapsed before new orders were received countermanding the retreat, but directing Baird instead to prepare magazines for the army on the road to Corunna; whereupon the division again advanced. The Brigade of Guards arrived at Astorga for the second time on the 14th of December, at Benevente on the 16th, and Mayorga on the frontiers of Leon and Castille on the 20th, where the flank companies were again incorporated with the battalions.

In the meantime, Moore, having marched from Salamanca on the 12th of December by Alargos and Toro, on the 20th December at last effected a junction with Baird's force at Mayorga, a point some ninety or so miles from Salamanca and approaching fifty miles from Astorga. Moore's army, consisting of 23,500

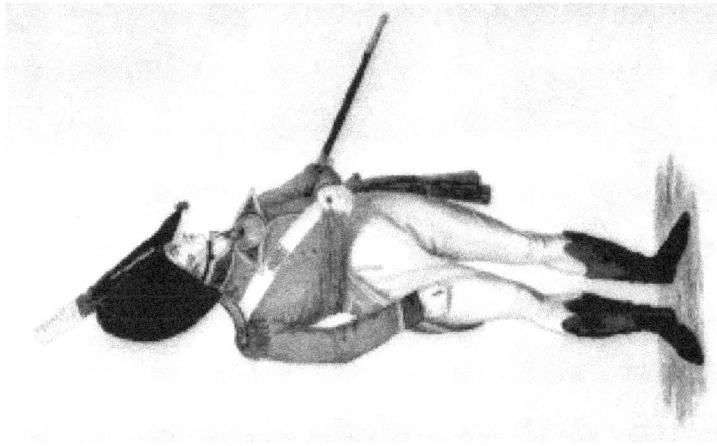

OFFICER OF THE FIRST FOOT GUARDS

FIRST FOOT GUARDS, 1807

infantry, 2,000 cavalry, and sixty pieces of artillery, was finally in one place under his command.

Before the union of the armies, Moore had intended, once they were combined, to retire his force on Lisbon, but at this point he changed his mind again (almost certainly influenced by considerations other than the logical or soundly military) and decided that the army could not leave Iberia without striking a blow (preferably useful) which might include a raid on Valladolid or even Burgos, though any operations in the vicinity of the latter city would take his army much farther away from the assistance of British ships at Corunna.

******

Moore Disney, now a brigadier-general, had as before mentioned, returned to Sicily at the beginning of 1808 in command of the Messina citadel and garrison until mid-April, when Sir J. Stewart arrived and took command of all the forces in the Mediterranean. Disney was ordered home to take command of a brigade at the end of July. He arrived at Lisbon on the 6th of October, in temporary command of a brigade of the line, consisting of the 2nd, 3rd, 6th, and 50th regiments of foot, with orders to join Sir John Moore's army. By the time his column had reached Castel Branco by the 27th of November, he received the intelligence that the British troops were going to retreat. Moore Disney was then given the command of another brigade (28th, 91st Regiments), forming part of the reserve, under Major-General Paget, so he left Castel Branco, and joined the main army at Toro on the Douro.

******

Warde had now resumed the command of the First Guards, and occupied a convent at Majorga. The right of the main army was on the 17th of December at Toro, with Moore Disney, his brigade of the line and the rest of the reserve, in front. Moore Disney continued his march northwards to Grajal on the 21st, two or three miles from Sahagun, which was then occupied by the Brigade of Guards. All of the army by this point had been marching about the country for almost a month.

The kind of opportunity for battle that Moore was hoping for then fortuitously materialised comparatively close by his own position. He had discovered that Marshal Soult was in an isolated position on the Carrion River in command of less than 20,000 men and so he proposed to surprise and defeat him before he could be reinforced. Matters began auspiciously as when the French advanced guard came into view, the 10th and 15th Hussars, under Paget, went forward, and drove the enemy's cavalry off the field. As the French held the bridge over the Carrion, the Guards Brigade, with the rest of Baird's division, were ordered on the night of the 23rd of December to prepare to attack.

Napoleon had already discovered the whereabouts of the British Army and had left Madrid in pursuit of it. Moore, in turn had learned the emperor was on his way at the head of a formidable army of approaching 45,000 men. The moment of crisis had arrived. Fully appreciating that he was not strong enough to take issue with the combined French armies and, with no expectation of assistance from the Spanish, Moore realised that his options had expired and that there was no time to lose. He immediately abandoned his plans for a battle and prepared for a retreat into Gallicia towards Corunna where the army could be evacuated by sea.

We may speculate upon the mood of officers and in the ranks in Moore's army at this juncture. The Spanish, until comparatively recently in league with the French, had failed, for one reason or another, to be remotely effective allies in the prosecution of a war that was principally their own. Indeed, there can be little doubt that the distrust, frustrations and ultimately contempt that the many of the British soldiers in Spain felt towards their Spanish ally began in this period and endured to the end of the entire conflict.

Moore's army had undergone long marches and its sole achievement, which was no stipulated part of its original mission, had been to create a diversion which had been conceived by Moore himself in the absence of any better alternative objective. Though this manoeuvre was undoubtedly of value (and the subject of some focus in retrospective positive consideration of Moore's expedition), it is not difficult to suppose this was considered by the army to be meagre recompense for all its efforts. Indeed, the price to be paid for Moore's military effectiveness was that he became a target for Napoleon's particular attention. When the emperor learned that the British Army had quit Salamanca he remarked, 'Moore is the only general now worthy to contend with me. I shall move against him in person', and so he did at the earliest opportunity.

Baird's force had marched long and hard only to be deprived, on the eve of a redeeming engagement, of a 'cut at the enemy' which would have justified their trials. Now in rough terrain and harsh weather the order had come to escape to save the army. British soldiers, in the main, did not do well with notions of impotence or in retreat in situations where they could not be held under the strict discipline upon which order depended and that augured poorly for what immediately lay ahead which was a gruelling march of some two hundred and more miles.

CHAPTER SEVEN

The Retreat to Corunna, 1809

Mid-winter in northern Spain was now hard upon the British Army. The Guards, with Baird's division, retired on Christmas Day by Valencia de Don Juan, and, preceded by the rest of the infantry, crossed the River Esla the next day, occupying Villa Manian, where they halted for two days to give the main body time to pass at Benevente. When the cavalry of the emperor's vanguard reached the Esla, Lord Paget, who would command the cavalry at Waterloo as the Earl of Uxbridge, turned back with his hussars, and cut to pieces the Chasseurs à Cheval of the Imperial Guard (December 29th), capturing Lefebvre-Desnouettes, their commander, and many of his men. The Guards reached Astorga, some twelve hours' march farther, on the same day, where Hope's and Fraser's divisions had already arrived.

The Brigade of Guards was lodged in the episcopal palace of Astorga. At four the next morning, Baird's division, preceded again by Hope's and Fraser's, was *en route* but the weather deteriorated rapidly and before long stragglers began to drop behind. After a halting progress, it was late in the evening before the column reached Manzanel, a small village surrounded by snow covered mountains but, at ten o'clock that night and before the men could find anything to eat, the retreat recommenced. Early on the New Year's Eve the troops arrived at Bembibre, where wine-cellars were broken into, looted of their contents and discipline in the army began to unravel as drunkenness became widespread. The weather was wild and storm driven, rain and snow had made the roads almost impassable, and numbers of the column increasingly perished by the roadside or were taken prisoners as they fell to exhaustion, inebriation or other reckless conduct.

Napoleon advanced towards Astorga just two days' march behind the rearguard of the British Army and eager to snap at its heels. However, at that moment, Destiny intervened at its most capricious, for the emperor received intelligence from France that the Austrians were about to return to the contest, inspired in measure by events in Spain which demonstrated that, contrary to hitherto widely held conviction, the French were demonstrably not invincible. Incisively aware, as ever of his priorities, the emperor abandoned his personal commitment to the destruction of Moore's army and returned immediately to Paris (where he also had domestic intrigues aplenty to contend with, in addition to the actions of his honestly declared enemies), diverting a large portion of the army from the pursuit to proceed to Madrid, Leon or central Europe.

Soult's command was now charged to trail Moore's increasingly demoralised, exhausted and bedraggled column alone and so bring it to account. Ironically, Moore was now retreating before the very commander he had intended, with some confidence and expectation of success, to defeat on the Carrion.

This turn of events had even farther-reaching consequences, for now Moore was not fated to fight a huge French Army under Napoleon at Corunna. The emperor's commanding presence and massive numerical advantage on that battlefield would certainly have increased the probability of a British defeat, ensuring the evacuation of the bulk of the army would be impossible. The political consequences of such an outcome had the potential to shake British Government resolve and craft future policies. The effect of such an outcome on the governments of the Continental nations needs no elaboration.

However, this also meant Napoleon was not fated, in 1809, to experience (and so profit from) fighting a desperate British Army in a defensive position under the command of an excellent general. He would only discover what that would be like, having in ignorance denied its unique qualities against the advice of those of his officers who knew it from bitter experience, on the afternoon of his downfall in June, 1815. It is on the turn of cards such as these, when converging paths fail to make their conjunction by mere hours, that empires fall and the fortunes of future centuries are dependent. As for the young Alexander Fraser, Lord Saltoun; irrespective of his eventual destination, we may safely speculate that he had more immediate matters and concerns on his mind at this time.

When the French cavalry again made contact on the 3rd of January, the army withdrew through Cacabolos where the rear guard formed at bay and the enemy were soon disabused of any thoughts that their quarry had lost its teeth or the will to bite when pressed. The artillery caused havoc among the advancing French horsemen and skirmishers of both sides were hard at work. It was here that Rifleman Plunket of the 95th made his legendary, long range shots to bring down General Colbert and his *aide*.

At the close of the action the army reformed column of route and trudged through Villafranca, where Moore had calculated that the pursuers would probably no longer follow him. The French pressed him continually however, forcing him on to Alilea, where the army arrived at about one in the morning of the 4th of January. At seven in the morning the troops were again *en route* for Santa Maria upon a steeply climbing road over the mountains which separate Leon from Castille. A thaw brought no relief and the already poor road became a quagmire of mud and filth, clogged with the ghastly, stinking detritus of war in all its forms; broken down carriages, dead horses and mules and the pitiful scattered corpses of men and women, their still shapes captured within a maelstrom of driving rain, sleet, and clawed by an unabating bitter, cold wind. Through it all the starving, fatigued and miserable column, heads down, continued its march.

On the 5th of January the army marched through Santa Maria to a rising ground beyond Constantine, and having failed to break up the bridge behind them, were closely harassed throughout the day by a strong body of French cavalry and *voltigeurs*. The 28th Regiment, under Disney, faced this encroachment and a few cannon shots dissuaded the French from further advances. According to a British witness during the retreat the French *voltigeurs* actually lived up to their literal appellation. These diminutive skirmishers were (theoretically) both able and intended to 'vault' onto the croup of a cavalry horse, the more quickly to be taken into action. Whether leaping was involved or not, they were regularly seen being carried by French cavalry, which was wryly noted in the British ranks since their own green riflemen had to march everywhere, yet nevertheless always gave good account of themselves.

The bullocks drawing the carts with the money-chests could now go no further and so, after something of an altercation as to what should be done with the money, 90,000 dollars were thrown down a precipice. In the evening the troops, having passed Nogales, arrived at Lugo, and took up a position in front of the town. When Marshal Soult's vanguard arrived in front of the British position, he opened fire on its centre, but soon discovered that the red ranks before him constituted more than a rearguard. After making a feint on the right, a column and five guns attacked the British left, but these were repulsed by some companies of the Guards and General Leith's brigade.

On the morning of the 8th the British Army was still in position about a mile in front of Lugo. Moore knew he could not afford to delay his departure any longer. Before quitting Lugo, he issued the following order:

> It is evident that the enemy will not fight this army, notwithstanding the superiority of his numbers, but will endeavour to harass and tease it upon its march. The commander of the forces requests that it may be carefully explained to the soldiers that their safety depends solely upon their keeping to their divisions and marching with their regiments; that those who stop in villages or straggle on the march will inevitably be cut off by the French cavalry, who have hitherto shown little mercy even to the feeble and infirm who have fallen into their hands. The

army has still eleven leagues (about 38 miles) to march, the soldiers must make an exertion to accomplish them; the rearguard cannot stop, and those who fall behind must take their fate.

The enemy army that followed the British was, of course, suffering the same debilitating weather conditions and was at this point barely superior in numbers, so could not afford to be less than prudent in its conduct. This does not imply any parity between the British and French armies at this point, for Soult's advantage was that he could march back into the Spanish interior to continue operations linked by lines of supply and communication in concert with other friendly forces whereas Moore, most decidedly, could not. However, at that moment both protagonists continued to doggedly march westwards, each commander carefully focussed on the actions of the other.

Shortly after nightfall on the evening of the 8th, the British Army quietly withdrew from its position and marching through Lugo, recommenced the retreat to the sea, leaving its bivouac fires burning in the darkness so that the vigilant enemy would not immediately learn it had slipped away. Once again, the weather broke and Paget's division, followed by the brigade of Guards and Baird's division, moved off in a terrible storm.

The first men in the retreat filled the buildings on the roadside to escape the deluge and had to be forced onwards. It was daybreak on the 9th before the Guards arrived at Vaamondas (now Baamonde), a little over twenty miles further on, where the army took up another position. Here the men lay scattered over a bleak and desolate heath with nothing to protect them, or lined ditches to escape the cutting wind and there many perished. Regiments became mixed together and stragglers continually dragged themselves in, though many were never seen by their comrades again. The respite was necessarily a short one and after a few hours' halt, the main body continued its retreat, arriving at Betanzos on the evening of the 9th of January after another punishing night and day. The toll on lives within the army during this period had been particularly heavy.

In the midst of the difficulties of this day's march, the Brigade of Guards preserved some order and discipline; the reserve covered the retreat, and these soldiers, who were in frequent contact with the enemy, nevertheless lost fewer men than succumbed in other regiments. It is, perhaps, understandable that those troops, who belonged to units renowned for especial *esprit de corps*, discipline or physical fitness, fared better in these extreme circumstances. A contemporary writer commented:

> The corps in which there was the least straggling were the artillery (who had ever a special regard for their guns), the Guards, and the reserve (which included the riflemen of the 95th and others). The Guards were the strongest body of men in the army, and consequently suffered least from fatigue; besides, they are strictly disciplined, and their non-commissioned officers are excellent.

On the morning of the 11th, Major-General Disney's brigade of the 28th and 91st Regiments was still forming the rearguard, and so was actively engaged in protecting the rear of the army at the bridge over the river at Betanzos, which they had in vain attempted to blow up behind them. The army continued its march on the 12th, in the knowledge that this was to be their last day on the road and, in the course of the day, it finally reached Corunna.

Sir Robert Arbuthnot later recalled that he was standing near Sir John Moore who was watching the troops coming in to Corunna, when Sir John called his attention to one particular column.

'Arbuthnot,' exclaimed Moore, 'look at that body of men in the distance. They are the Guards, by the way they are marching.'

'It was a fine sight', Sir Robert recalled, 'and one I shall never forget. We watched them and saw them march into Corunna by sections, their drums beating, the drum-major in front flourishing his stick, the sergeant-major at the head, and the drill-sergeants on the flanks keeping the men in step, exactly as if they were on their own drill-ground at home'.

The first and third battalions of the First Guards, with the rest of Baird's and Fraser's divisions, occupied the town itself, while

Hope's division was quartered in the suburbs, and the reserve at El Burgo.

Chapter Eight

The Battle of Corunna

The British Army that arrived at Corunna was in a parlous condition. An eyewitness recalled:

> The soldiers lay scattered about, wearied and dispirited, ragged in their dress and many of them sickly and broken down by the fatigue of the retreat. Most of their chins had been untouched by a razor for days, perhaps weeks, and their faces blackened by the smoke of their muskets and the charcoal of their cooking fires.

Moore's divisions, approaching 15,000 strong, after two days' rest, moved on the 14th from their quarters in the town and took up their positions for the coming battle on a ridge about two miles from the town. The British position and its objectives were simple. Behind the army, formed in a defensive arc, lay the town and sea. In the harbour would lie the ships of the Royal Navy and the means by which the army might be excricated. The French would attack to prevent that escape and the British would attempt to defeat the French so that it might safely evacuate the majority of the army.

The advantage of motivation demonstrably lay with the British Army which was fighting to save itself, but it fared better than might be initially imagined compared to the French Army, since it had rested, now had the advantage of numbers and had been substantially resupplied. Few lessons are original and Soult was about to be taught one as old as humankind, which is that one should mindful of what one elects to chase for one may ultimately catch up to it.

Baird's and Hope's divisions were formed in line; Baird's on the right, and from the direction of the ridge, obliquely approaching the enemy's position, so that a great battery on the French left enfiladed it. The Guards, under Sir Henry Warde, were in column in support of Baird's right, this being the weak point of the position. Fraser's division was posted a short distance in rear of the Guards, while Paget with the reserve was in rear of the centre.

The long-awaited transports arrived, entered the harbour of Corunna and had begun to load the stores of the army together with the greater part of the artillery. Before the infantry could embark, however, there was a battle to be fought. At about two o'clock on the 16th, the French Army under Soult, advanced in three columns, covered by skirmishers, against the British position; attacked the left column, carried the village of Elvina, and thereafter dividing, one wing attacked Baird directly in front while the other wing attempted to turn his right flank. If this attack had succeeded, the destruction of the British Army would have been inevitable. The 4th Regiment on the right of Baird's line was thrown back on its left, and opened a flank fire on the advancing French column, while Paget's reserve descended into the valley in order to check its further advance.

The 42nd Highlanders and 50th Regiment, forming the right centre of Baird's line, then advanced and stormed the village of Elvina. Baird received a bullet in his arm, which forced him to leave the field, and Sir John Moore, observing that an gap was left in the line, by the advance of the 42nd and 50th regiments, sent orders to the brigade of Guards instructing it to move forward and occupy the village. The first battalion of the First Guards deployed and advanced down the hill to the assistance of the regiments in Elvina with the third battalion forming in support.

As Major Henry Hardinge (later Governor-General of India at the time of the First Anglo-Sikh War and Commander-in-Chief of the British Army during the Crimean War), who had

THE FIRST FOOT GUARDS AT CORUNNA

carried the order to the Guards to advance, was reporting to Sir John that the French cavalry had been repulsed, Moore was struck by a cannon shot which carried away his left shoulder and part of his collar bone. Upon his falling, the command of the army devolved to Sir John Hope.

The reserve on the extreme right overthrew the French column, and approached the great artillery battery on the French left. The British left wing also repulsed the attack made upon it. The tide of the battle had turned and the British advanced driving the French force before it. By five o'clock, the enemy was confining itself to a long-distance cannonade as it disengaged and by six o'clock Soult was unequivocally retiring. The opportunity to destroy Moore's army had not been taken when it was at its most exposed and debilitated and so the battle that was fought by the French at Corunna came too late with too few resources to achieve a positive outcome for them on the field.

The mortally wounded Sir John Moore was carried off the field by six soldiers of the First Guards and 42nd Highlanders and brought into Corunna, where he died in the course of the evening. He was interred in the north-east bastion of the citadel, by the side of his friend Brigadier-General Anstruther, formerly of the Third Guards, who had commanded a brigade during the retreat, but who died on the day the army reached Corunna. The funeral service was read by the Rev. Symonds, one of the First Guards chaplains.

The retreat to the ships commenced at ten o'clock at night with the exception of the brigades of Generals Hill and Beresford, which remained as a rearguard to cover the embarkation, and the majority of army, including the Brigade of Guards, boarded their ships during the night. Hill and Beresford's brigades embarked the following day, harassed by French artillery from a battery brought on to a height commanding the harbour.

The muster-rolls of the First Guards revealed that the first battalion had only lost five men and the third battalion eight killed on the day of the battle. However, during the following weeks, the first battalion lost a further eighty-six men and

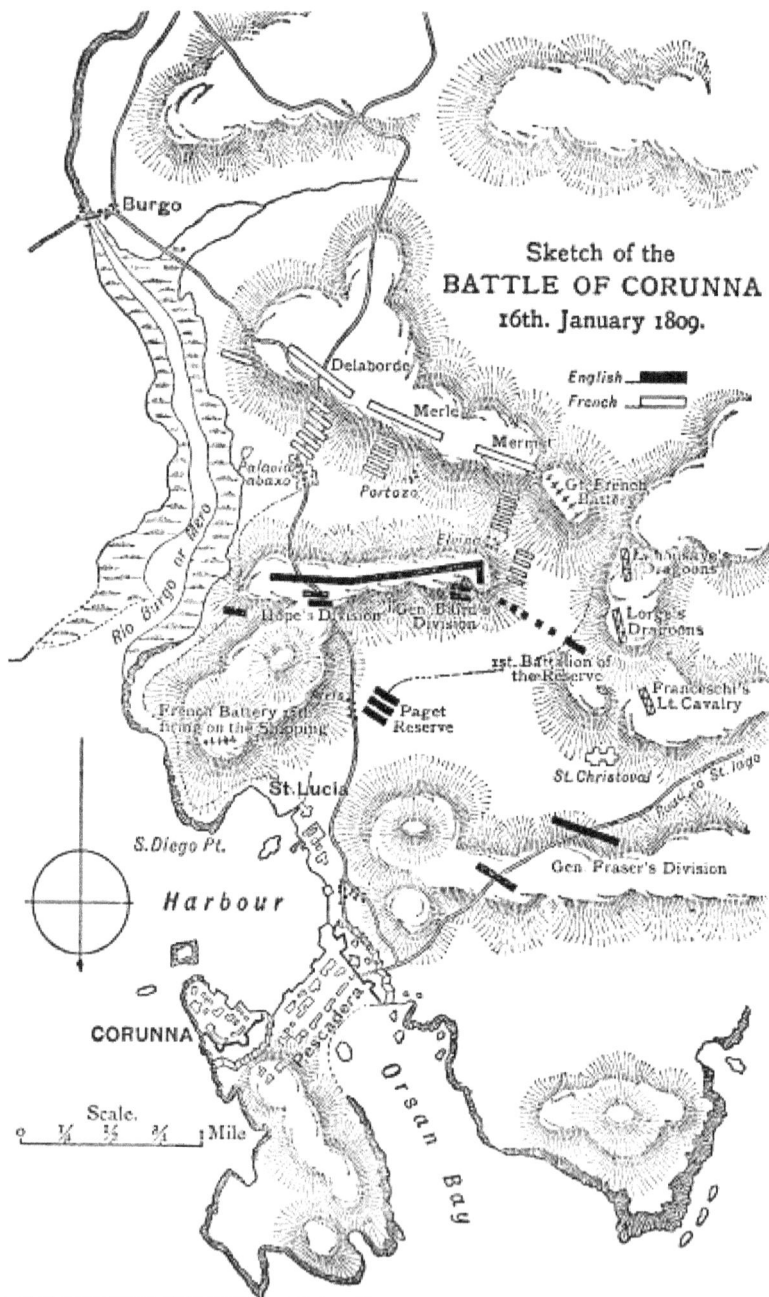

Sketch of the
BATTLE OF CORUNNA
16th. January 1809.

English
French

Burgo

Delaborde

Merle

Mermet

Gt. French Battery

Palavia baxo

Portozo

Elvina

La Houssaye's Dragoons

Rio Burgo or Mero

Hope's Division

Gen. Baird's Division

Lorge's Dragoons

1st. Battalion of the Reserve

Franceschi's Lt. Cavalry

French Battery first firing on the Shipping

Paget Reserve

St. Christoval

Road to St. Iago

St. Lucia

S. Diego Pt.

Gen. Fraser's Division

Harbour

CORUNNA

Pescadera

Orsan Bay

Scale.
0 ¼ ½ ¾ 1 Mile

the third battalion fifty-four men who died as a result of their wounds, sickness or fatigue. Sixty-nine men of the first battalion and fifty-six of the third battalion were taken prisoner by the enemy during the retreat. The total loss to the British Army during the campaign, including the advance, the retreat to Corunna, and in the subsequent action, was in the region of 4,000 men,(Oman says 6,000) of whom 800 subsequently found their way to Portugal and where they were formed into battalions of detachments.

Moore's last words were that he hoped his nation would do him justice which suggests that he had a presentiment that it might not do anything of the kind, for a victory at the end of a hard retreat and on the eve of an evacuation would never qualify as unequivocal good news from which credit would be attributed to the commander who had presided over the affair. Military reverses usually require someone to have blundered and blamed so, justified or not, the pointing fingers of accusation were inevitable.

That having been said, Moore came to realise his situation was hopeless, that he would get no assistance from the Spanish and so he could not fulfil the intentions of his mission. He made it clear in his last letter writing that 'as a military man I should have retired from Salamanca'. He possibly should have been on his way before that time or at least soon after his arrival at Salamanca for the 'writing was on the wall' early in his expedition and nothing then occurred which might have encouraged him to believe that his situation would improve.

Notwithstanding his clear appreciation of his harsher realities, Moore, aware that he would be appraised as a 'military man', then concerned himself with the intangibles of honour and the politics of perception and those distractions were his undoing. Considerations only matter before the fact. Thereafter, uncompromising verdicts upon outcomes are delivered by everyone with the inclination to voice an opinion. Since Moore was now dead, he could no longer appeal his case even if, had he lived as unlikely as it would have been, he had been inclined to do so.

Moore admitted that he was disappointed with the conduct of the army during the retreat, but that behaviour was always likely to surface in the British Army of the day on campaign when it broke lose, for whatever reason, from the strict bonds of discipline that held it together. The Duke of Wellington could attest to that fact as readily as could Sir John Moore, for he also had no remedy for widespread disorder among the ranks before the fact and in extreme circumstances could only regain control of disorderly soldiers driven by drink, lust and rapacity with the threat and application of the lash and the gallows.

We may speculate whether Wellesley would have fared better than did Moore in his shoes. Certainly, he would have found himself in the same position as regarded his Spanish allies for little changed in that respect during the time he was commander-in-chief in the peninsula. Both generals were talented and resourceful tacticians who could have depended on the army to perform well under their direction when it came to fighting, for then it was in its element. In fact, had he not fallen at Corunna, Moore would have probably attacked, driving the French into the River Mero which lay at their backs.

However, based on what we know of Wellington, we might believe he would have marched for the ships when he realised it was the only viable solution, irrespective of other considerations, for he repeatedly demonstrated in the peninsula that he was ever the pragmatist, manoeuvring the army (advancing or retreating, with no discarnate luggage attached to either direction) until he arrived at the right place, at the right time, to realise his immediate objectives. Indeed, Wellington not only continued to employ this very methodology to position the army in the last great battle he fought, but also applied the same principle during his subsequent political career, including in circumstances where, in the absence of bloodshed, it was seen to be an unacceptable *volt-face* on matters of policy.

Alternatively, aware of his disadvantages in Spain, Wellesley may not have stuck his neck out quite so far as Moore had done in the first instance, though in either event he would certainly have drawn the emperor's attention upon himself at which time the distance between the British force and Madrid would have become critical to any outcome.

Be that as it may, Sir John Moore's death made a change in the command of the army in the Peninsula certain for good or ill and his place would be, in due course, taken by another general. That man, as it transpired, would be Arthur Wellesley who was shrewd enough to know that the campaign fought against the French revolutionary armies in the Low Countries was 'precisely how not to conduct a campaign' and so able to learn, if that was necessary, the lessons that Moore's campaign taught any commander who might find himself in a similar position.

As the Duke of Wellington, he would ultimately demonstrate he was the right man, possibly, though irrelevantly the better man, for the challenges that lay ahead. In fact, as the First Guards sailed back to England another British Army was making its way towards the Iberian Peninsula and ere long Wellesley would join it as its commander. The regiment had earned its first battle honour in the Peninsular War, 'Corunna', for their battle had been won, if the campaign had not.

CHAPTER NINE

The Return to Portugal, 1809

The homeward bound fleet encountered a storm which scattered the convoy and actually wrecked some vessels, but the transports which carried the First Guards came through it all unscathed, anchoring safely in Portsmouth harbour on the 25th of January. The troops returned to their barracks at Chatham where they received numerous transfers from the second battalion, which was garrisoned in the capital, in the course of the Spring months. The evacuation from Corunna may have been the end of an episode, but the war against Napoleonic France was far from over and so before the end of that summer, the Guards would yet again be sent on foreign service.

Meanwhile, after the British had sailed away from Spain, Soult's command, unimpeded by opposition, returned to Corunna to re-establish the French grip on the region, concentrating in the vicinity of the port for about a month. Having rested, the marshal and his force then struck southwards, marching on the city of Oporto in Portugal, which was stormed in late March.

The British Government had already realised that it would be necessary to dispatch reinforcements to the Peninsula and so at the end of the year 1808, had assembled another expedition under Major-General Sherbrook to join the forces already in place, about 9,000 men, under Cradock. This force comprised the Second Brigade of Guards (Coldstream and 3rd Regiments) under Brigadier Henry Campbell of the First Guards, together with the Irishmen of the 87th and 88th Regiments. This expedition sailed in the middle of January, 1809, and so, of course, ran into the same gales that beset the homeward bound fleet carrying the First Brigade of Guards from Corunna. Adverse weather conditions kept the fleet at Cork in Ireland for a month, arriving eventually in Spain at Cadiz, where the Spanish authorities were as usual obstructive, though in the event orders arrived from England ordering the transports to Portugal.

So, the fleet moved on towards the mouth of the Tagus, landing the Second Brigade of Guards in the vicinity of Lisbon in the middle of March. The remainder of the troops of the line regiments which had served under Sir John Moore were also sent back to Portugal as soon as they had recruited replacements, together with other additional reinforcements sent out from England. In February General Beresford had been sent out to reorganise the Portuguese Army, amply accompanied by numbers of British officers to assist him, with a huge supply of new arms and equipment.

Sir Arthur Wellesley arrived in Lisbon on the 22nd of April, assuming not only military command from Cradock (who had in the interim showed little enterprise, though had at least, provoked no disasters), but supreme authority in the country. Wellesley had over 28,000 British and German troops (some admittedly *en route*) and 15,000-16,000 Portuguese at his disposal. This was yet another comparatively small army with which to oppose the numerically superior French presence in the region, given it was almost certainly going to be required to depend upon its own resources.

Nevertheless, Wellesley had boldly asserted, contrary to Moore's views, that with a British Army of 20,000 or 30,000 men and the control of the native forces, he would hold Portugal against any French Army not exceeding 100,000 men. The British Government elected to take the gamble that he was right. The new general had arrived at an opportune moment for the French invasion had come to a standstill. Marshal Soult would not move without reinforcements from Marshal Ney, and Marshal Victor would not move without reinforcements from Madrid.

Wellesley, appreciating the potentials of this isolating procrastination, saw he could deal a blow at either Soult or Victor, while leaving a detached force to 'contain' the other.

He resolved to deal with Soult first leaving 12,000 men at Abrantes to watch Victor and given success, he then intended to move swiftly to Estremadura to deal with the second French Army. The army crossed the River Douro near Oporto in the face of Soult's army on the 12th of May. Such was the marshal's surprise at this development that he left his dinner on the table in his haste to be away, whereupon it was appreciatively devoured by General Rowland Hill's divisional staff. Hill established himself in the town, while Sherbrook's, division with the Second Brigade of Guards, consisting of the first battalions of the Coldstream and Third regiments, under Campbell, threatened the enemy's rear. Comprehensively wrong footed, Soult was compelled to retreat over the mountains to Braja and Orense, losing his artillery and baggage, and 5,000 men on the way.

Wellesley followed up this blow, as planned, by marching against Marshal Victor and thence on Madrid, joining with the forces under the Spanish general, Cuesta. The army then advanced on the 22nd of July to Talavera, and on the 28th fought a bloody battle in which the French attack was completely defeated, and for which victory Wellesley was created Viscount Wellington. Tellingly, on examining the thin line of redcoats before his attack, Victor had proclaimed, 'If we do not enforce this, we should give up the war'. The British general then turned northwards towards Soult, but finding that the French marshal had 50,000 men at Navalmoral, he prudently retired to Almarez and Merida, in Estremadura, where the army went into cantonments.

Wellington could have had few illusions, based on his initial experiences in Iberia and re-enforced by what he had learned of Sir John Moore's campaign, that he could rely on co-operation or support from the Spanish authorities, generals and armies. The defence of Portugal and the success of the British Army

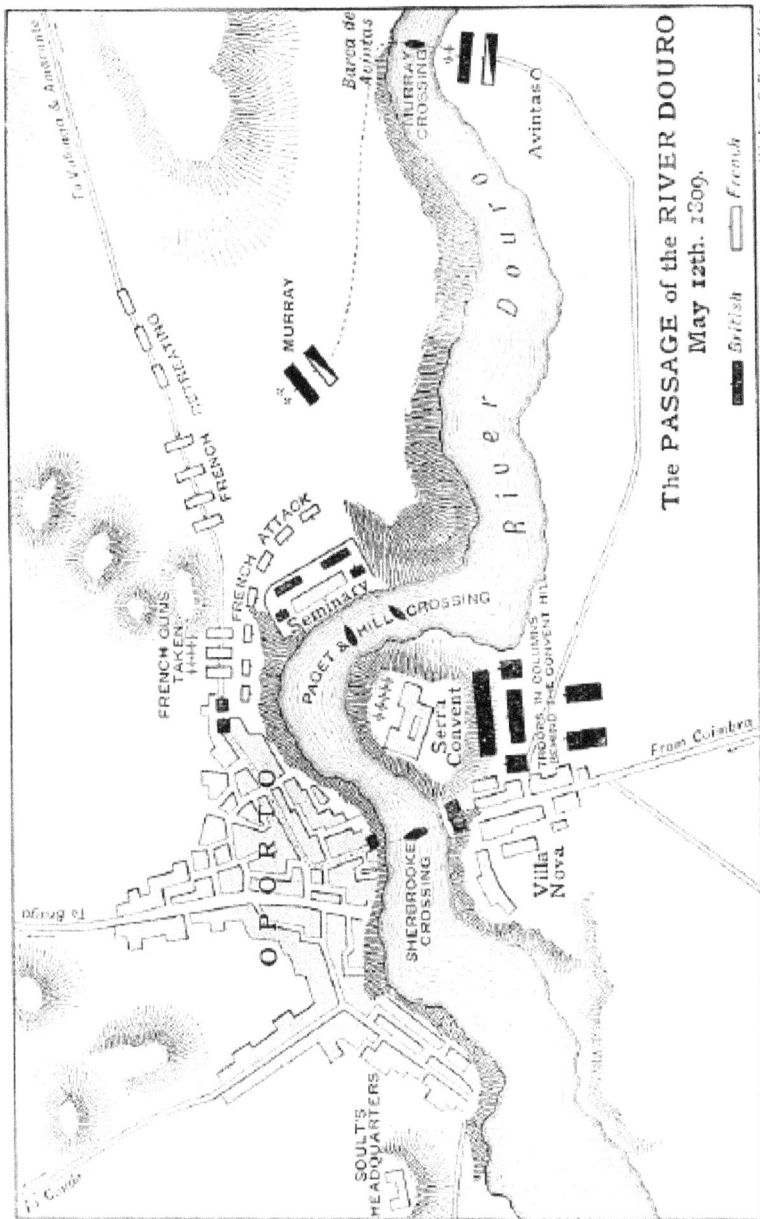

The PASSAGE of the RIVER DOURO
May 12th. 1809.

British ▭   French ▬

River Douro

Barca de Avintas

MURRAY CROSSING

Avintas○

From Coimbra

To Valonga & Amarante

To Braga

MURRAY

FRENCH RETREATING

FRENCH

FRENCH GUNS TAKEN

FRENCH ATTACK

Seminary

PAGET & HILL CROSSING

OPORTO

SOULT'S HEADQUARTERS

SHERBROOKE CROSSING

Villa Nova

Ser'a Convent

TROOPS IN COLUMNS BEHIND THE CONVENT HILL

S. Garda

in Spain must, therefore, depend on his own judgement and those resources of any kind over which he had authority, though indirectly the Spanish armies continued to be of assistance by their very existence which required the attention of numbers of the French who might otherwise have been entirely employed against the British. However, it is not the purpose of this narrative to describe the activities of the Spanish armies.

Aware that the time would inevitably come when his army, given its modest size and in the absence of support by Spanish armies, would find itself faced by a French force of superior numbers in the field, Wellington determined that he would not find himself in the same predicament that had so fatally compromised Moore. There would be no retreat to the sea in the expectation of waiting transports and another precipitate evacuation courtesy of the Royal Navy.

A large safe haven on the Iberian Peninsula itself was needed which could accommodate the entire army in addition to a civilian population. All parties would be required to sustain themselves and thus the means to be readily resupplied. That no such initiative was instituted during the period of Moore's campaign cannot be laid to that general's account for that would have required a foresight that nobody at that time had demonstrated they possessed.

The Portuguese capital, Lisbon, sitting upon the tip of a broad peninsula flanked by the ocean and the River Tagus was the ideal location for Wellington's enterprise, for the river is accessible to maritime traffic and leads towards safe anchorages. Accordingly, Wellington directed the construction of the formidable and virtually unassailable defensive works across the landward approaches to the city which became known as the Lines of Torres Vedras and, furthermore, ordered forts to be built so they might defend the wide mouth of the Tagus from enemy incursions from the water.

Behind these lines, not only could the army and populace find safety, but be indefinitely supported by sea whilst an enemy force, deprived of the means to live off the land, would not only remain impotently excluded but, if disinclined to retire, eventually be the architect of its own dissolution.

However, since we are principally following the First Guards and Alexander Fraser, Lord Saltoun we must leave the Peninsular War for the struggle with Napoleon's France was being fought on other fronts in the summer of 1809 and a plan was formulated for an expedition to the the Low Countries. The two battalions of the First Regiment lately returned from Spain were ordered to hold themselves in immediate readiness to join this force and, unfortunately for the third time in this conflict, the guardsmen were on their way to a place where affairs would not go favourably according to plan.

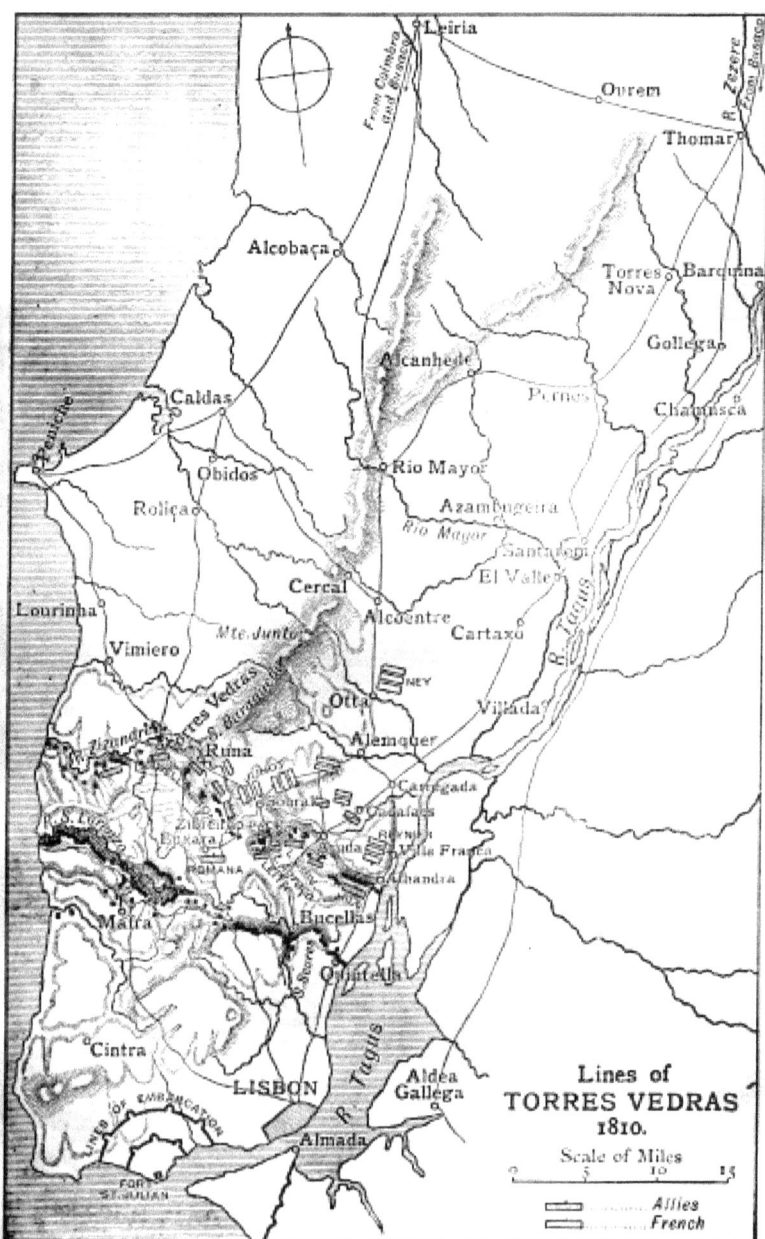

Lines of
TORRES VEDRAS
1810.

Scale of Miles

| 0 | 5 | 10 | 15 |

Allies
French

CHAPTER TEN

The Walcheren Expedition, 1809

Whilst the British Government was aware that the imminent danger of a French invasion launched across the English Channel had been averted, it felt a potential threat against the British homeland somewhere from the sea remained. Of particular concern to it was the French concentration at Antwerp in the Low Countries.

The Scheldt waterway gave access to the seaways from that city and provided secure maritime passage, anchorages and shipyards as it flowed between the main land and the oddly shaped peninsula of North and South Beveland with Walcheren on its western extremity. Antwerp, at the farthest eastern reach of the Scheldt (before it becomes a river of usual proportions), provided a secure base for the French Navy, removed from coastal waters and so inaccessible to enemy warships at sea. The city also supported a sizeable military arsenal.

The British view was that this 'pistol at the head of the country', on its left flank should be neutralised, but in any event it was hoped a robust attack launched from the west would also create a diversion which could provide some relief for Austria and others who were opposing Napoleon in central Europe. In retrospect, this initiative had the hallmark of 'someone's bright idea', for the Scheldt is some distance (compared to the width of the English Channel) from England's shore and so enemy ships would be exposed for some time (during which they would be vulnerable) to the attentions of the Royal Navy which dominated the seaways. Simply put, given Napoleon knew he could not cross to England without risk of disaster from Boulogne/Calais, (1805), why would he then attempt a crossing from Antwerp (1809)?

Nevertheless, in late May the British Government determined the time was right for a pre-emptive strike. Antwerp was poorly garrisoned, some of its troops having been withdrawn to reinforce the *Grande Armée* engaged on the Danube. An ambitious plan was conceived to capture or destroy the enemy's ships wherever they could be found between Antwerp and Flushing, destroy the Antwerp, Terneuse and Flushing arsenals and dockyards and reduce Walcheren. Ideally the Scheldt would then be made no longer navigable for ships of war, after which the army was to return to England, leaving a garrison on Walcheren. The fleet was to be commanded by Admiral Sir Richard Strachan and the army would be under Lieutenant-General, the Earl of Chatham.

The First Brigade of Guards, the first and third battalions of the First Regiment, now commanded by Major-General Moore Disney, received orders to embark on the 23rd of July; and the flank companies of the three second battalions, forming the Third Brigade of Guards, were also ordered to join the expedition. The total strength was 109 officers and 3,091 men. The two battalions of First Guards were under the command of Colonel William Anson and Colonel George Cooke respectively, with Lieutenant-Colonel Hon. Philip Cocks and Lieutenant-Colonel Kelly as seconds in command.

The army, 21,000 strong, was organised in four divisions, under Lieutenant-General Sir John Hope, the Earl of Rosslyn (who had assumed command at Corunna after the death of Moore), Lieutenant-General Grosvenor, and the Marquis of Huntly. The size of this expeditionary force is noteworthy, particularly compared to the forces that had been dispatched to Portugal and Spain thus far, though of course, the Low Countries were closer to home than the Iberian Peninsula and the perceived enemy threat one that bore directly on Britain itself.

Lord Chatham proposed the establishment of a base in a strong position from which to launch further operations, on the north side of South Beveland. From that point the enemy's batteries could be taken in the rear, forcing the French fleet, which was off Flushing, to move up the river, for fear of having its line of retreat cut off. This would allow the approach of the British fleet to Flushing. Hope's division, which was the reserve of the army, was selected to be the military component of this operation and was composed of the Brigade of Guards under Disney, the first and second battalions of the 4th and 28th regiments under the Earl of Dalhousie and the 20th, 92nd and Vet. Battalion under Erskine totalling 7,261 effectives. Admiral Sir Richard Keats commanded the transporting of this division, and as it was to precede the rest of the army, it sailed from the Downs on the 28th of July. The Earl of Chatham, with the other divisions, set sail on the 29th and 30th.

The grenadiers and First Battalion, First Guards, and other regiments of Hope's division, were taken some distance up the river in boats and landed without opposition on the morning of the 1st of August, on the north side of South Beveland at a point between Wilmenduye and Cattendyke. The grenadiers of the Guards, and a detachment of the 95th (Rifles) then moved forward towards Cloeting. Strong patrols were pushed towards Goes, whilst leaving three companies of infantry of the 20th Foot at Cattendyke. Goes capitulated, occupied by the 92nd Regiment and the enemy retired towards Batz.

The Guards remained that day at Capelle and Boulingen, and Erskine's brigade at Hexendenkinder and Goes. The Third Battalion of Guards did not land until the following day, the 2nd of August. The division already on shore, again advanced, the Guards towards Vaarden, the 4th Regiment to Hanswardt. The grenadiers of the Guards then pushed on to Kruyningen, there surprising seventy or eighty of the enemy and making them prisoners without loss to themselves.

The Dutch evacuated Vaarden, and subsequently, on the 4th of August, as the British continued their advance, abandoned the town and important fort of Batz, on the low ground opposite to and commanding the entrance of the Scheldt. The Guards then took up a position between Cattendyke and Batz. It came as something of a surprise to Hope that this fort, considering its strength and position, should be so readily given up without resistance since it was manned by some 600 troops.

Nevertheless, passage was now free for the fleet between Walcheren and South Beveland, so Hope stressed the importance of naval support near to the fort. This was not, however, forthcoming and its absence was soon felt, when on the 5th and 8th of August the enemy began to heavily bombard the fort from twenty-five gunboats. Whilst the bombardment was at its most intensive, Grenadier John Skinner, performed an act of extraordinary bravery. Under fire, Skinner un-spiked twelve guns that had been spiked and abandoned by the French in Fort Batz with tools he made himself so that they were able to be turned upon the enemy gunboats.

Eighty guns and a quantity of ordnance stores had fallen into the possession of General Hope's division. On the 9th of August the Earl of Rosslyn's division landed on South Beveland, when, as senior officer, the earl assumed the command. While operations against Fort Batz were taking place, the troops under the immediate command of Lord Chatham had landed, on the 30th of July, at Veere. They came ashore on the north-east shore of the island of Walcheren, without opposition after the fire from the mortar and gunboats had driven the enemy from their defences.

The town of Camour was cannonaded, and soon surrendered, and on the 4th of August Fort Rammekens was taken by General Fraser. The flotilla could now advance, preventing enemy relief from being thrown into Flushing, which was subsequently invested. After a bombardment, which set the town in flames, it also capitulated. The garrison marched out having been granted 'the honours of war' on the 18th of August.

After the fall of Flushing, Lord Chatham, with his headquarters, moved to Goes, in South Beveland, and subsequently to Fort Batz, joining Sir John Hope's division with the Brigade of

WALCHEREN CAMPAIGN, 1809

Guards. About this time the most dangerous enemy the British troops would encounter began to make its appearance, in the form of a debilitating fever, 'occasioned' as contemporary sources referred to it in an all-embracing term of medical ignorance, 'by the fatal miasma arising from the inundations'. It is now widely accepted that what beset the troops was a lethal cocktail of malaria, typhoid, typhus and dysentery which would lay low many more soldiers than bullets and become the defining feature of the expedition.

The first part of the operation having been eventually accomplished, the proposed attack on Antwerp was the next and final objective, but Louis Bonaparte, a younger brother of the emperor and King of Holland since 1806, had in the meantime arrived with reinforcements and Bernadotte had assumed the supreme command of the French troops.

The strength of the enemy in Antwerp was now about 11,000 men; between Antwerp and Bergen-op-Zoom, a further 15,000; and in Bergen-op-Zoom, Breda, and Tholen, and on the left bank of the Scheldt, 11,000 more, making a total of 37,000 men either in or within striking distance of Antwerp. The effective force of the British Army was about 30,000 in total, but if the siege of Antwerp was undertaken, 6,000 of them would be required to remain in Walcheren, and 2,000 more remain in South Beveland. It would also be necessary to mask Bergen-op-Zoom and Breda; 10,000 or 12,000 men would be required to cover the siege, leaving only 10,000 men for the siege itself. Simply put, the practicability of the initial plan of the expedition had demonstrably unravelled.

The admiral, Sir Richard Strachan pronounced that the fleet could not move higher up the Scheldt as long as the two forts of Lillo and Liefkenshoek, situated on opposite sides of the river, half-way between Fort Batz and Antwerp, remained in possession of the enemy. The navy, Strachan conceded, would co-operate with any attack upon them, but taking them would necessarily be a task for the army. He further stressed that time was pressing and supplies in the fleet were running low especially of fresh water, so immediate action, was to take place, if it was required.

It is clear from Lord Saltoun's letter to his mother despatched at this time that he was already aware that the useful service of the army in this operation was over, which rather suggests that there were few, if any, officers in the British force who were unaware of it. He writes, as one might readily expect, of the sickness that plagued the army, but notably that the Guards suffered less from it than other troops and one may speculate this was a consequence of their general fitness and the high standards maintained in all things, including cleanliness, within the regiment. The contents of his missive reveal, once again, that Saltoun was both well informed and astute. However, this letter appears to suggest, since he makes no reference to it, that he was not sick himself at this time or previously. We may readily speculate why, in writing to his mother, that may have been the case. His nephew, the 17th Lord Saltoun, from a perspective of intimate knowledge, in his writings provides more illumination on that subject by informing the reader:

> Lord Saltoun did not escape the terrible Walcheren fever, caused by malaria, that proved fatal to so many, from the effects of which even his iron constitution suffered in no slight degree during future years.

We may assume that the 'Ross' referred to in the last paragraph of this letter was John Ross, a lieutenant-colonel of the Coldstream Guards who had been killed at Talavera in the previous month. He was 65 years old at the time of his death, had seen service dating back to the Seven Years' War and had fought with Butler's Rangers in the Mohawk Valley during the American War of Independence.

South Beveland,
August 26th, 1809

Dear Mother,

Since I last wrote you we have remained in the same situation; the headquarters have been moved from Walcheren to this island, and the other day they came down to Batz, near where we are, and with them I was in hopes they would have brought our letters, and given us some opportunity of writing home; but not in the least, and we are likely to return without any opportunity of either hearing from or writing to England.

It is now the general opinion that the business is at an end, and we shall shortly retrace our steps, as the enemy have in their hurry and confusion on our first appearance inundated the country between Bergen-op-Zoom and Lillo, as well as that on the left bank of the river, which renders our further progress, if not impossible, at least attended with such difficulties and loss, as would be greater than the taking of Antwerp is worth, and it is therefore concluded that we shall either move to some other part of the enemy's coast or return home; in case of the latter a large force will most probably be sent to Spain, and I should not wonder if the brigade of Guards were amongst the number. The army in general, officers as well as men, have been very sickly; the complaint is an intermittent fever, attended with much giddiness in the head. I never remember, even in the worst of times in Spain, so many sick as we now have in the brigade, and we are much less so than the rest of the army; the worst is that it seems to be a complaint of the country, and they are not likely to get better as long as they remain in it.

There has been a council of war sitting all day, and has not as yet broke up; it will most probably determine what is to become of us. Montague Wynyard of the Coldstreams, who has got his promotion by the death of Ross in Spain, is just going home, and will take this with him. I think we shall soon follow.

I am, dear mother, your dutiful son,

Saltoun.

Love to all at home.
27th August 1809.

A memorandum, on the increased strength of the hostile forces compared to the British, was submitted to the generals for their consideration. Its disconcerting contents required little deliberation on their part and they came to the inevitable conclusion that the siege of Antwerp was impracticable, and so that there was no advantage to be gained by the reduction of the Fort of Lillo, or from any other operations in the vicinity. The expedition was at an end and South Beveland was evacuated.

By early September no troops were left in the Scheldt, except a small garrison at Walcheren, under General Don positioned to prevent the enemy's fleet escaping from the river. He then received orders to evacuate the island, and after destroying the basin of the harbour and naval defences, his force embarked for England in mid-December

The First Brigade of Guards had already landed in England at the beginning of September, and moved to their former quarters. In his history of the Grenadier Guards, Hamilton informed his readers:

> They had suffered much from sickness, both officers and men bringing with them the seeds of disease from which many suffered to the latest hour of their lives; none had fallen in action, but many a grave was filled from the 'Walcheren Fever' contracted in this fruitless campaign.
>
> By a return made out five months later, at the beginning of February, 1810, it appears that, of the ninety-one officers of the First Guards, one died of fever on service, and two on their return, all of the first battalion; and that of the 2,574 non-commissioned officers and men of that regiment, twenty-one died on service, and 208 on their return. In the whole army no less than sixty-seven officers and 4,000 men died of the fever, and at the date of the report in February above 200 officers and 11,000 men were still in hospital.

The Walcheren Expedition was a failure, made the more poignant since nothing like the threat that was the inspiration for it ever materialised (nor was likely to do so) and it, furthermore, achieved nothing which might have been assistance to the Austrian war effort. Most modern military history students would throw up their hands upon reading the mission brief, for it was too complex; over reaching in its objectives and required significant distances to be traversed, given there were points of contention to be reduced along the way, before the ultimate objective was reached, much less won. Unfortunately, most military students can bring to mind similar plans made in more recent times.

The notion that the army could finally quit Walcheren and

return to England leaving behind a garrison that could endure to be influential for the longer term was fanciful. Essentially, the expedition's best chance of success would have been an effective raid in force (in effect a demonstration of intent and capability) which would inflict the maximum damage in the face of least resistance in the minimum amount of time, before promptly withdrawing.

The motivation for the operation was the intelligence that the ultimate objective, Antwerp, was insufficiently defended by the enemy at the time. At no time could it have been assumed that Antwerp would not be strengthened by the enemy (whose presence dominated western continental Europe) as readily as it been depleted of troops and that single consideration ensured 'time' was the principal command consideration for the British operation. Had the operation been more limited in its goals and shorter in the time allocated to its execution, it is probable the incidence of sickness would have been much reduced, though one could not expect that any military planner of the period would have been aware of the likelihood of 'Walcheren Fever' much less have made provision for it before the event.

That accepted, any degree of success depended upon the joint military and naval commanders effectively co-operating in perfect co-ordination without delay and in the absence of the caution that may have been appropriate in a campaign of longer duration. This simple requirement was demonstrably beyond their grasp to conceive or implement, though apparently it was clear to contemporary British commentators, for at the time an epigram began to circulate extensively enough to become well known.

The Earl of Chatham, with his sword drawn,
Was waiting for Sir Richard Strachan:
Sir Richard, longing to be at 'em,
Was waiting for the Earl of Chatham!

In the words of Alexander Fraser, the 17th Lord Saltoun:

The French and Dutch strained every nerve to assemble a superior force for the protection of Antwerp. Sickness of a most fatal description broke out in the British ranks, and the opinion of the seven lieutenant-generals of the army having been taken towards the end of August, further progress was decided to be impracticable.

Napoleon, as has been explained, left his marshals to prosecute the war in Spain, and found on his return to Paris that Austria was, indeed, about to resume hostilities. The emperor had, of course, lost none of his talent for the waging of war and beat his enemies at Landshut, Eckmühl, and Ebensberg and was, by mid-May, once more in Vienna. He crossed the Danube, but was beaten at Aspern-Essling, though not decisively, so he needed only to withdraw to the island of Lobau in the Danube. In early July of 1809, the French resumed the offensive and fought the Battle of Wagram. This was a bloody affair for both sides, but the Austrians were eventually obliged to retire.

The Austrians called for an armistice, which led to a peace treaty ratified in Vienna in October. The emperor had once again, for a time, prevailed and though the Austrians were temporarily cowed they were not conquered and that outcome in Napoleon's campaigns was becoming a perpetual problem to France. Napoleon's enemies were several, their resources massive and they remained prepared to oppose him. By contrast his allies were few. The allegiances of many of them were more compelled than willing and so begrudging in their affiliation. Others would eventually become disillusioned as they became aware that there was little substance to French promises. The War of the Fifth Coalition was over, but the glimmer of hope ignited in Spain had grown brighter at Aspern-Essling and so it was a certainty that before long hostilities would renew in northern Europe.

As for the Walcheren Expedition, it was unnecessary, ill conceived, poorly executed and would probably have brought few rewards of worth had it been successful. The high loss of life among British troops as a consequence of 'Walcheren Fever' served to transform a blunder into a tragedy.

EVACUATION FROM WALCHEREN

CHAPTER ELEVEN

The Siege of Cadiz, 1810

The invasion of the southern provinces of Spain had been delayed for a time by Sir John Moore's diversionary tactics in 1808, though the value of those manoeuvres was demonstrably confined only to the period during which they were being carried out. The south of the country was spared again by Wellington's march towards Madrid after the Battle of Talavera but, once again, the subsequent British retreat into Portugal (where the Lines of Torres Vedras were soon to prove themselves an insurance policy more than worth the cost of its premium) cleared a way for the French, which they consolidated by defeating the Spanish Army at Ocaña, thirty miles south east of the capital, on the 16th of November, 1809.

If Seville was to fall, as surely it must since there was no force on the peninsula to oppose it, then the road for the French was open to the valuable harbour at Cadiz on the Atlantic coast. Though the fortress at Cadiz was ostensibly formidable, very few guns were mounted on its ramparts, whilst the garrison consisted only of a few thousand Spanish militia who were undoubtedly not equal to the task of holding the place against a concerted French assault.

Notwithstanding its indisputable vulnerability, the British had always been aware of the importance of preventing the French obtaining possession of the fortress and harbour of Cadiz, and so had sent General Sherbrooke there in the Autumn of 1808 with 4,000 men, and Major-General Mackenzie followed him with a brigade in February, 1809, but neither of these expeditions actually landed to take up the task, being recalled for the more pressing requirements of the defence of Portugal.

The situation was, on the face of it, looking grim for the allies in the Peninsula at this point for nowhere were their fortunes in the ascendant. Napoleon had been diverted from Iberia by the resurgent Austrians, but that matter, as has been explained, was now settled—at least for the time being. The emperor accordingly focussed his attention once again on Spain and Portugal making his intentions unambiguous by massively reinforcing the French presence in the theatre.

In 1810 Napoleon felt he was faced with two options for the direction of his principal offensive efforts in the region. The first was the subjugation of Andalusia and the second was to overwhelm Wellington's army and drive the British out of Portugal once and for all. He decided, probably correctly so far as he was in a position to judge the matter, to prioritise the first option since it represented the line of least resistance. The emperor calculated that the destruction of the British Army could be postponed until 1811, amply demonstrating (for the British Army) the legitimacy of the phrase, 'It is an ill wind that blows nobody any good'. Unfortunately for Napoleon's schemes, a Spanish general in Andalusia was about to display an act of good judgement and timely energetic resolution and the British general who would be required to do nothing, but obligingly await the hour of his own destruction was Wellington.

The French Army in the south of Spain was now under the command of Marshal Soult. Both Cordoba and Seville were predictably captured and Cadiz then appeared to be within his grasp. It seemed probable that the Spanish Army of the south was about to be driven into the sea, for the passes of the Sierra Morena had been forced at three points and the demoralised troops under Areizaga had dispersed or fled eastwards into Murcia. The Duke of Albuquerque meanwhile retreated westwards by forced marches and with 8,000-10,000 men threw himself into Isla de Leon, near Cadiz, in early February, 1810.

Marshal Victor however, was swiftly following the Spaniards, reaching Chiclana, within a few miles of Cadiz, only two days afterwards and on the 10th of February he summoned the town to surrender. That demand was promptly rejected, so the French began an investment, establishing lines which surrounded the bay. Rota, Santa Maria, Puerto Real, and Chiclana were fortified, and entrenched camps established in essential positions, the principal one being at Chiclana, near Barrosa. The First Guards would, in due course, take part in the long defence of Cadiz which lasted from February 1810 until late August 1812, becoming one of the most important sieges of the entire war.

A deep inlet of the sea, the Santa Petri, was the first Spanish line of defence; the second was the Isla de Leon, an irregular triangle, the apex called Torregardo, pointing to the city, the base resting on the Santa Petri, the right on the harbour, the left on the sea. The Isla, which was about seven miles long, and half a mile broad, was marshy, except a ridge four miles in length, on which the town of La Isla stood. A narrow isthmus about five miles long connects Cadiz with the apex, and across this isthmus was a cut called the Cortadura, defended by the unfinished fort of Fernando. Wellington expressed an opinion that, 'If the Isla was lost the town would not, and probably could not, hold out for a week'.

A tongue of land projected from the eastern shore of the harbour, and separated the inner from the outer harbour; this tongue was divided by a canal called the Trocadero and at the extreme point stood the fort of Matagorda, opposite to which, at 1,200 yards' distance, on the isthmus leading to Cadiz, stood a powerful battery called Puntales. From Cadiz to Matagorda was 4,000 yards and from Matagorda the French could completely command the upper or inner harbour, as well as the fort of Fernando. Wellington visited Seville in December, 1809, and had drawn up a memorandum advising the completion of the work on the isthmus about Cortadura, in order to secure the communication between the Isla and the town. He also recommended the construction of another strong work at the Torre d'Ercole (Torregorda).

On receiving information of the French advance upon Cadiz, Wellington despatched Major-General Sir William Stewart with 2,000 men comprised of the 79th, 84th, and 89th regiments to assist in its defence. This brigade arrived on the 11th of February, and was soon joined by a Portuguese regiment 1,300 strong. The British Government also decided to dispatch Lieutenant-General Graham from England with an additional reinforcement of 5,000 men, of which a portion of the Third Brigade of Guards under Major-General Dilkes of the Third Regiment formed a part. The remainder of the Third Brigade was to be left in England.

Early in March six companies of the Second Battalion, First Guards, under Colonel Sebright, and three from each of the second battalions of Coldstream and Third Guards, under Lieutenant-Colonel Onslow, left London for Portsmouth; embarked on board their transports and were landed at the Isla de Leon on the 24th of March, with the rest of the reinforcements under Graham, who immediately assumed the chief command in the Isla, where all the allies were quartered.

Fort Matagorda, which had been dismantled by the Spaniards, was hurriedly reconstructed to provide a serviceable defensive position, but after an obstinate fifty-four days contest, its isolated position revealed that holding it was untenable. At the end of April it was abandoned to the French, who promptly occupied it, but although they held the fort for over two years, were never able to make good use of it. The defenders were able in turn to constantly subject it to their own accurate and well-directed fire. The British force in Cadiz had been raised in July to 8,500 men, but in October, a hard-pressed Wellington sent for some of the regiments, reducing the garrison to 5,000 troops. Before the close of the year, however, it was again reinforced from Gibraltar and Sicily.

CADIZ.
AND ITS ENVIRONS.

SCALE OF YARDS

High Road to Seville

French Camp

French Camp

French Camp

French Camp

Chiclana

Salt Marshes

Spanish Camp

Punta de Santi Petri

Castello de Santi Petri

ISLA DE LEON

Spanish Camp

Isla

Bridge of Suazo

Arsenal (La Carraca)

(Salt Marshes)

Torre Garda

to Arcos

Puerto Real

INNER HARBOUR

Fort San Luis

Grapeshot

French Camp

Fort San Jose

Matagorda R

Fontaine Castle

Cortadura

Puntales Castle

San Luis

Castle of S. Sebastian

Cadiz

OUTER HARBOUR

"Usual position of Fleet"

Castle of Santa Catalina (Ruined)

Guadalete R.

to Xeres

Puerto de Sta. Maria

Telegraph

From San Lucar

Rota

The French tried hard to conclude their assault, including from the water by the imaginative use of 130 gunboats which had come down the River Guadalquivir and had then been transported overland on rollers from Santa Maria to the Trocadero Canal. Huge mortars, which threw shells 5,000 yards, were also employed by the French, but only an occasional shell plummeted into the city, creating much alarm among the population, but doing little actual damage. Soult's first objective was to overpower the fire of Fort Puntales, and establish himself between the Isla and the city, but as long as the allies held the great redoubt of Cortadura, General Graham considered the communication secure from interruption.

This was the state of affairs at Cadiz at the close of 1810, in which the six companies of the Second Battalion, First Guards, besides three from each of the other regiments, all under Dilkes, were employed in the defence. The city continued to be accessible by sea, but on its landward side the French continued their blockade.

The French had opened the campaign of 1810 in June in Iberia by the besieging of the Spanish held walled towns of Ciudad Rodrigo and Almeida on the Portuguese border, both of which soon surrendered, and in September, Masséna, at the head of 60,000 French troops, advanced into Portugal. Wellington responded with a retirement which brought his forces to a strong position on the heights of the Sierra de Busaco. The French marshal engaged him on the 27th of September, but his attack was comprehensively repulsed and his troops driven down the mountain in a battle that, once more, pitted defensive line against attacking column, contributing to the catalogue of Wellington's triumphs fought, 'in the same old way'. Nevertheless, Masséna then succeeded in turning the British left, and Wellington continued his retirement towards his secure base of Lisbon.

On the 10th of October, 55,000 British and Portuguese troops passed into the Lines at Torres Vedras and defied the following French to breach them. Masséna examined every feature in the entire line of defences to discover a potential weak point but, so comprehensive were they, he found none. Weeks of impotent exclusion dragged by and the French position not only failed to improve, but grew progressively worse since the country had been laid waste to ensure the marshal could not benefit from it. His own army's supplies soon began to dwindle and, without the means to replenish them, hunger began its cruel work. Winter was approaching and with it came rain and outbreaks of sickness among the French troops. Accepting the inevitable, Masséna eventually turned away from Wellington's army, secure in its warm billets, and marched his own miserable soldiers into winter quarters in the vicinity of Santarem. The historian, Professor Charles Oman, suggested that from this turning point the fortunes of the French in Iberia were ever in decline and he wrote:

> The offensive power of the French hosts in Spain was spent; and it may be said that the retreat which began at Santarem only ceased at Toulouse.

Meanwhile far to the south, in the first weeks of 1811, the apathy of the Spanish authorities with regard to the siege of Cadiz remained conspicuous and while General Graham praised the exertions of the British engineers and soldiers who toiled to improve and extend the defensive works, he complained that the Spaniards, always in part the architects of many of their own misfortunes, endeavoured to prevent the execution of some of the essential measures required to secure the defence of the city.

CHAPTER TWELVE

The Guards at Barrosa, 1811

In January,1811 the allied commanders attempted to force the enemy to raise the siege of Cadiz, encouraged by the absence of Soult and his Fifth Corps which had been diverted for the siege of Badajoz. The offensive plan required the creation of a combined force of Spanish and British troops which would embark on ships and land in the vicinity of Tarifa, behind the concentration of the enemy, so it could fall upon the rear and flank of the comparatively modestly sized French Army of the First Corps under Victor in camp at Chiclana.

Meanwhile, a Spanish force in the Isla was to throw a bridge over the San Petri and threaten the French lines in front. The allied force destined for this operation amounted to 14,000 men, of whom about 4,300 were to be British and allied soldiers including a component of Guards. In reality, the Anglo-Spanish Army was probably not quite large enough for the task in hand given an expectation of certain success.

The British contingent consisted of a battalion from Gibraltar made up from the six flank companies of 1/9th, 1/28th, and 2/82nd regiments of Foot, eight companies of the 28th from Tarifa, whilst Cadiz provided the Guards, the 2/67th and 2/87th foot, the flank companies of the 2/47th Foot, six companies of the 95th Rifles and two light companies of the Portuguese 20th regiment. The cavalry element was two squadrons of the excellent 2nd Hussars of the King's German Legion. Artillery support was provided by 10 guns under the command of Major Duncan and totalling about 4,314 men.

The Brigade of Guards, under Dilkes, 1,221 strong, with a detachment of the riflemen of the 95th regiment embarked at Cadiz, sailed to Algeciras, disembarked and marched westwards towards Tarifa on the 28th of February. Command of the British contingent was held by the able Lieutenant-General Thomas Graham who, (given the experiences of the past regarding co-operative efforts in concert with the Spanish Army), uncharacteristically and, as it transpired, unwisely waived claim to overall command of the operation. That responsibility was conceded, probably for the usual intangible political reasons given the disparity of numbers of troops from each allied nation involved, to the Spanish General, Don Manuel de la Peña.

The long column of the army advanced on the 2nd and 3rd of March *via* Casas Viegas and Vegas de la Frontera, and, with the Spanish element in the lead, about noon on the 5th of March reached the heights of Barrosa, which are situated four miles from where the River San Petri joins with the sea. The ridge of Barrosa stretched about a mile and a half from the coast, being bounded on the left by cliffs, on the right by the Forest of Chiclana, and in front by a pine wood. Beyond this there rose a narrow height called Bermeya, which could be reached by moving through the wood or along the beach under the cliffs.

The troops had marched twenty miles all through the night to reach their objective and were exhausted. La Peña, nevertheless, pushed forward sending the Spanish vanguard to the mouth of the San Petri, where it joined forces with the troops on the Isla. General Graham was then directed to follow the vanguard, but could immediately see the error of such a course of action and strongly advised La Peña against it, emphasising that since it was certain the enemy would imminently make an appearance, it was imperative that the British force take action to hold the commanding position of the ridge.

Graham was well aware that the advance of the Allied Army to its present position could not be a surprise to Victor who was, indeed, essentially waiting for the arrival of the Anglo-Spanish column to present him with his best opportunity to deliver a decisive attack. Neither force, likely to be brought to the actual battlefield, possessed an influential numerical superiority, though Victor could draw upon a further 6,000-7,000 men which were dispersed along his entire line. Furthermore, and fortunately for Graham, Victor had considerably over estimated the size of the Allied Army; an error which governed his own manoeuvres. Prudence, therefore, in every decision was essential to avoid a defeat which would inevitably be far more problematic for the Anglo-Spanish Army than for the French.

Graham's judgement, which transpired in every respect to be correct, was however, over ruled by La Peña and so in obedience to his orders Dilkes's brigade of Guards and Wheatley's brigade, marched off to the left in front and over the heights, leaving only the flank companies of the 9th and 82nd Regiments, under Major Brown, together with the baggage, in an untenable position on the hill and facing overwhelming opposition. Almost incomprehensibly, no sooner had Graham entered the wood than La Peña, having sighted and been overawed by a body of French troops on his flank, led off his Spaniards by the sea-road to San Petri leaving the Barrosa ridge unprotected and covered with baggage.

The French in the meantime were intently watching these movements from the Forest of Chiclana, and Marshal Victor, observing the opportunity presented by the separation of the Allied Army, promptly advanced onto the plain with 7,000 or more veteran soldiers and fourteen pieces of artillery. A Spanish guerilla guide informed Graham that the enemy were coming round the wood and were on the plain they had just quitted. The Brigade of Guards, under Dilkes, was immediately faced about. The Second Battalion, First Guards, which was in front, formed line to the right, the men filing into line under a galling fire as they came out of the wood. The three companies of the Third Guards, under Barnard, were formed in support in a second line, while Wheatley's brigade, with whom were the three companies of the Coldstreams, under Colonel Jackson, were told off to cover Duncan's guns, formed on the left.

When General Graham debouched into the plain, he discovered the high ground key of the position had fallen to the French, the Spanish rearguard in full-flight heading towards the sea and no sign at all of La Peña. The situation was demonstrably desperate, for the British force was not only isolated, but barely constituted half the numbers their enemy had the potential to deploy. Graham, whose instincts were always inclined towards the aggressive and, in any event, seeing no alternative open to him but to assume the offensive, rode forward and waving his hat, reportedly cried out to his troops, 'Now, my lads, there they are, spare your powder, but give them steel enough.'

Covered by the fire of Duncan's guns, the little army advanced. Dilkes, with the Guards and part of the 67th Regiment, forming the right wing, marched rapidly against the French General Ruffin's column, bringing up their right shoulders on the march, while Wheatley's brigade advanced against the right of the French under Laval. The Guards had to cross a deep hollow, under a severe fire, before they could close with the enemy. They came up its farther side in loose skirmishing order and, without stopping to reform, rushed up the hill and crashed into the French upon its crest where the fighting became severe and, for a time, the outcome indecisive.

Ruffin fell mortally wounded; Sebright, commanding the Second Battalion, First Guards, also wounded, was carried off the field, at which point Colonel Sambrooke Anson assumed the command of the battalion. Brigadier Dilkes had his horse killed under him, but the Guards and their comrades resolutely drove forwards delivering an 'incessant slaughtering fire,' of musketry from their line and driving the enemy columns before them.

Wheatley's brigade on the left was equally successful; a determined charge of three companies of the Coldstreams and Gough's, Irishmen of the 87th Regiment overthrew Laval's first line, driving the French 8th Regiment, whose eagle was captured by the 87th, upon their second line, whereupon the broken columns of the French began retiring from the field. They made one more attempt to turn, but Duncan's guns forced them to continue their retreat, and the British troops, who had been twenty-four hours without food, were unable from sheer fatigue to pursue them further. During the whole day 'no Spanish soldier fired a shot nor drew a sabre' to assist their outnumbered allies. This short but fierce battle lasted but an hour and a half, and in that time approximately 1,200 British and in excess of 2,000 French combatants were either killed or wounded.

The casualties in the Second Battalion, First Guards were two ensigns, two sergeants, thirty-one rank and file killed. One lieutenant-colonel, three captains, four ensigns, eight sergeants, 169 rank and file wounded; total, 216 casualties. The officers killed were Ensign Commerell and Ensign Eyre, acting *aide-de-camp* to Colonel Wheatley. Of the eight wounded, six were severely wounded namely Lieutenant-Colonel Sebright commanding, whilst Captains Stables and Colquitt were very severely wounded as were Ensigns Sir H. Lambert, Cameron, and Vigors. The detachment of Second Battalion, Coldstreams had three ensigns and fifty-three rank and file killed or wounded; Second Battalion, Third Guards, three officers, ninety-nine rank and file killed or wounded.

Brigadier-General Dilkes, commanding the Guards Brigade, afterwards made his report on the engagement and the following is an extract from it which describes the action from his perspective with the usual formality which disguises the extent of the achievement of the British force in gaining an incredible victory in the face of superior opposition.

> About two hours after the reserve had been ordered to halt in close column on the east side of the heights of Barrosa, on the morning of the 5th of March, I received Lieut.-General Graham's orders to proceed, together with Colonel Wheatley's brigade, towards Santi Petri—this was done, and the column began its march left in front over the height, and descending the other side entered a conifer wood, so thick as to be nearly impracticable for the guns and mounted officers. Having advanced about a mile, N. Reade, a staff-officer, overtook me, seeking General Graham, informing me that the enemy had made his appearance

on the heath or plain we had quitted; the deployment was soon after effected under all disadvantages (the detachment battalion forming a second line to the 2nd battalion of First Guards). At this time an application being made for a party to cover the guns, I sent three companies of the first-mentioned battalion for that service.

The line was advanced obliquely to the right, towards a body of the enemy already occupying the heights we had lately passed over, a heavy fire of artillery and musketry being kept up on both sides; but our line continuing to advance, I may say with distinguished gallantry, that part of the enemy's force immediately opposed to us withdrew towards another corps on his right. Our army still advanced, bringing up their right shoulder, and threatening his left, so that at last he formed that flank *en masse*, continuing his retreat down the hill, and ascending another rising ground, halting occasionally and keeping up a severely destructive fire. When fronted at one time, I perceived him push forward two or three divisions from the *masse* as I conceived, to charge our line, whose well-directed fire still advancing, obliged him to desist. Unfortunately, our men were so completely exhausted by their march, &c. &c., as to be quite unable to return the compliment.

That Graham had fought and won a gem of a battle which demonstrated the mettle of British troops under skilled leadership was beyond dispute. Wellington, who had a refined appreciation for a well-managed engagement, unreservedly declared 'admiration of the principle of the attack, and of the distinguished bravery which won the battle.' That having been said, there was never any point in an expedition from the besieged Cadiz, venturing out with all the risks that entailed, only to return to its lines without achieving its purpose which was to relieve the city by defeating the force which constrained it. That final outcome was the more galling not only because the affair had so closely come to catastrophe, but most especially because with the engagement of about one third of the available Anglo-Spanish force employed for the task it had, nevertheless, come so close to success.

Graham remained for some time on the heights waiting for

BATTLE OF BARROSA

La Peña, however despite all his urgent entreaties the Spanish general refused to send him cavalry reinforcements or even to take up the pursuit of the routed French force. Indignant and disgusted with the conduct of his ally, Graham at last led his own wearied troops to the Isla. La Peña came within the walls two days later and the two generals 'embarked on a campaign of intense wrangling' for all the good, after the fact, that could do. The hard truth was the expedition had the means within its grasp to wreck half the French lines, but had come back a failure having achieved nothing of value but military laurels for Graham and his soldiers. However, once again the British had been given a hard lesson on what they might expect (or not expect) when acting in concert with a Spanish Army in the field, and this fundamentally influenced the decision to take no further offensive action from Cadiz during the following months.

Shortly after the army returned to the Isla, Colonel Wheatley rejoined the Second Battalion, First Guards, and assumed the command, but owing to the severe losses it had sustained during the Barrosa expedition, it was ordered home. The third battalion of the regiment, commanded by Colonel G. Cooke, now completely recruited from the severe losses it sustained in the Corunna campaign and during the Walcheren fiasco, received orders in March to embark for Cadiz to relieve their second battalion comrades. With this battalion, Alexander Fraser, Lord Saltoun would return once more to the Peninsular War.

Six companies of the third battalion accordingly marched from London for Portsmouth on the 2nd of April, and disembarking at Cadiz on the 27th, occupied the St. Helena barracks. Two days afterwards General Graham inspected them on the glacis, at which point several men of the second battalion, who were selected to remain at Cadiz, were incorporated into the third battalion. The embarkation for England of the remainder of the second battalion, was delayed till the 4th of May,

The final four companies of the third battalion left London, embarking at Portsmouth on the 30th of May and, sailing in the middle of June, reached Cadiz on the 23rd. On their ar-

BARROSA

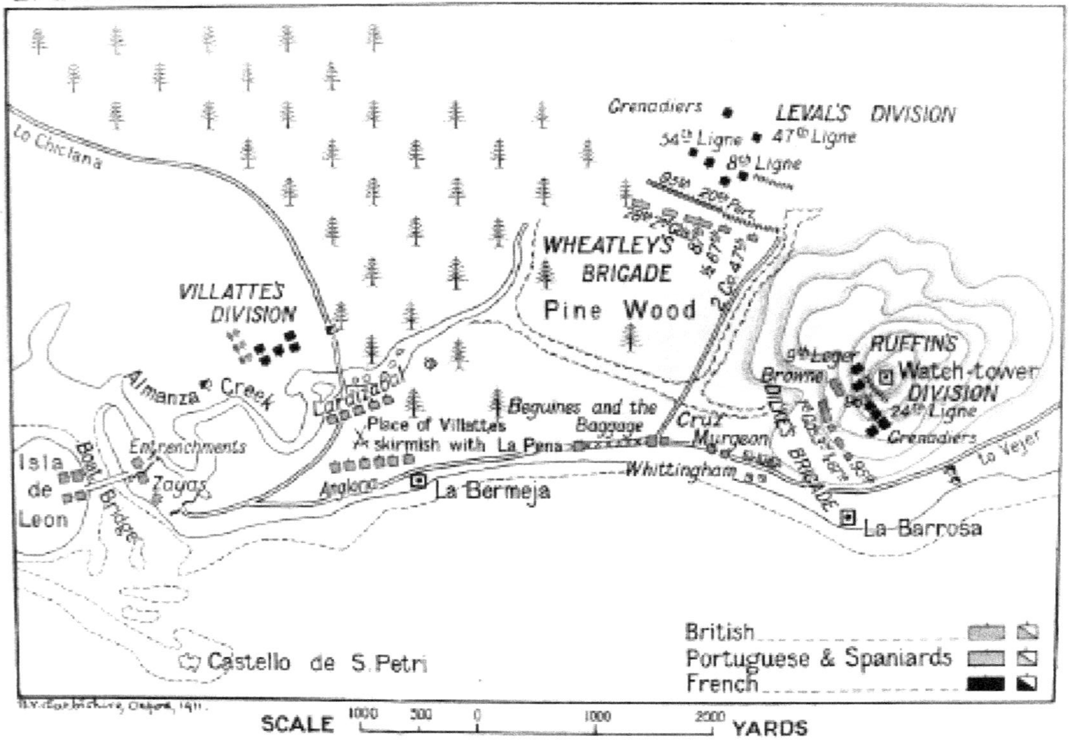

Grenadiers
LEVAL'S DIVISION
54th Ligne
47th Ligne
8th Ligne
WHEATLEY'S BRIGADE
Pine Wood
VILLATTE'S DIVISION
Lo Chiclana
Almanza Creek
Begunes and the Baggage
Cruz
Murgeon
Place of Villattes skirmish with La Pena
Entrenchments
Zayas
Isla de Leon
Boat Bridge
Anglona
La Bermeja
Whittingham
DILKE'S BRIGADE
RUFFIN'S DIVISION
Watch-tower
9th Leger
Browne
24th Ligne
Grenadiers
Lo Veyer
La Barrosa
Castello de S. Petri
British
Portuguese & Spaniards
French
SCALE
1000
500
0
1000
2000
YARDS

rival Colonel George Cooke, commanding the battalion, was promoted to the rank of Major-General, and placed on the staff, and Colonel J. Lambert took command of the third battalion. At the same time, Major-General Dilkes returned home. During the summer of 1811, Graham, was also removed to the command of a division in the field under Wellington, and was at first succeeded by Major-General Moore Disney, First Guards, but he then returned home in November, and the command at Cadiz eventually devolved upon Major-General George Cooke, First Guards.

Long unresolved sieges tend to become very dull affairs with little to do for the besiegers or the besieged. The duties of the Third Battalion, First Guards at Cadiz underwent very little variation in the course of the year. The construction of a redoubt was entrusted to them, for which purpose they found eighty men daily, while a detachment of seventy-five men, relieved weekly, was stationed at Cantera. The monotony of the siege was occasionally relieved by a bombardment from the French lines, but no attempt was made to storm the entrenchments. The siege of Cadiz became most problematic for the garrison in view of the continual friction that existed between the Britons and the Spaniards enclosed within the walls.

Lord Saltoun, who had arrived in the spring of 1811 with the third battalion, wrote a letter home from Isla de Leon, written 22nd of September 1811, in which he related an instance, from his perspective, of typical jealousy and misconduct on the part of the Spanish authorities.

> You say I do not send you any politics, the fact is there is nothing going on here but the old story; the Spaniards make no efforts themselves and lay all their losses to the fault of the English government and generals.
> Mutual dissatisfaction had been brewing a long time, but did not openly break out till after the Battle of Barrosa, in which, notwithstanding it was clearly proved that the English Army saved the whole of the Spanish Army and the Isla de Leon; notwithstanding that two of their own generals, namely, Sayis and Ladizabal, were so convinced that we had gained a com-

plete victory, that they repeatedly urged La Peña to advance on Chiclana; although General Graham offered to advance on Chiclana if they would support him, which they declined; yet the Spanish government countenanced a false account of the action, which was published by General Lacy, the head of their staff (a runaway rascal who had been turned out of the French service), in which he gives the whole merit of the action to the Spanish Army, denies General Graham's statement, and attributes the failure of the general plan to the ill-judged attack (as he calls it) that the English made.

This produced a correspondence between them, and General Graham obliged him to eat his words. Lacy had been put under arrest after the Battle of Barrosa, but, soon after this statement made its appearance, was reinstated in his rank and command; this of course created an open rupture between our heads of departments and the Spanish Government, which is likely to continue, at least as long as things go on in their present style.

The mass of the people and the army are with us, and if we were to offer them our pay, we might revolutionise the place in three days; but that is not our system. So much do the Spanish Government fear this, that false accounts are circulated, in order that the people may not be acquainted with the extent of their obligations to the British, and to excite, if possible, a jealousy between the two nations. They yesterday ordered away four thousand men, against which our minister remonstrated very strongly. Some of the troops, however, marched yesterday evening. Whether they will embark or not I know not, but if they do, our force will not be sufficient to defend the place, as our works are now become very extensive; but we must do the best we can, and I do not think the French will attack.

The reference to the apparently infamous General Lacy in Saltoun's letter is not without some interest. Luis Roberto de Lacy was the son of an *émigré* Irish soldier who had been in Spanish service. In 1811 he was 36 years old and serving in the Spanish Army in charge of a portion of the Cadiz defences. His career had, indeed, been chequered for he had fought against the French with the Royal Spanish Army, been jailed for duelling and maintaining a feud and dismissed, but then joined the

French Army serving with the Irish Legion.

He then deserted the French as they invaded Spain and re-joined the Spanish Army as a colonel. By 1813 he was Captain General of the Kingdom of Galicia. He opposed the return of King Ferdinand VII as an absolute monarch, after the end of the war in Iberia, following the king's *volte face* on the subject of a Spanish constitution, and in 1817, led one of the several failed coups. He was captured, sentenced to death and in July of that year executed by firing squad on Majorca.

The only other event of importance in this part of the campaign during this period was the defence of Tarifa in December, under Colonel J. B. Skerrett; Colonel Lord Proby, First Guards, being second in command. The successful result of this defence was mainly owing to the persevering skill of General Sir Charles Smith, of the Royal Engineers, which eventually caused the French under Victor to raise the siege of Tarifa, on the 4th of January, 1812. In the same month, an expedition under the command of Colonel J. Lambert, of the First Guards, was sent to Carthagena, though in April, he returned to Cadiz.

CHAPTER THIRTEEN

Operations in the Peninsula, 1811-12

Soult had captured Badajos from the Spaniards on the 10th of March, 1811, and Masséna was driven out of Portugal in the same month, but, upon hearing that Wellington had marched south, he advanced again to relieve Almeida, then besieged by the British. Wellington, however, suddenly returned and met him at Fuentes d'Onoro, which developed into a hard-fought contest in and around the village which, after two days, compelled the French to retire.

In the meantime, Marshal Beresford having invested Badajos on the 8th of May, Soult advanced to its relief, and Beresford encountered him on the 15th of that month on the ridge of Albuera, where one of the bloodiest contests of the war took place. The French were, however, defeated though at enormous cost. Soult now united his army to that of Marmont, who had superseded Masséna, and their superior forces compelled the British to raise the siege of Badajos. The French marshals, however, soon separated again, and during the remainder of the year, Wellington, manoeuvring brilliantly, maintained himself on the frontiers of Portugal. Soult returned to Seville, and General Hill, after surprising Gerard at Arroyo del Molinos, was left undisturbed in Estremadura.

Wellington invested Ciudad Rodrigo in the month of January, 1812, and after twelve days it was taken by storm. The truculent, General Robert Craufurd of the Light Division, so memorable from Moore's retreat to the sea was killed. Among

Scale 1 : 2,200,000

English Miles

the officers of the Guards, Captain Hon. James Stanhope, of the First Guards, who, as *aide-de-camp* to Lieutenant-General Graham, was present at the siege of Ciudad Rodrigo, was wounded on the 14th of January.

Wellington then moved south to Badajos, which fell after a siege of twenty-one days, though once again the British suffered appalling losses in the assault. Having now two large fortresses to secure his communications, Wellington crossed the Agueda and advanced against Marmont, who retired to Salamanca. After several days spent in manoeuvring, the hostile armies encountered each other on the 22nd of July. The ever-observant Wellington, detecting that Marmont had blundered in extending his left and weakening his centre, fell upon him, gaining a decisive victory. The French fled in confusion, and two eagles, six colours, sixteen guns, and thousands of prisoners were taken.

The enemy retreated in the direction of Burgos, and Wellington moved on Madrid, entering the capital on the 12th of August, before moving to the attack of Burgos, and orders were at once sent to General Hill, in Estremadura, and General Cooke, in Cadiz, to now take up the offensive.

Whilst the war in Spain continued on its positive course for Wellington, Napoleon, as always, was playing the grand game of empires elsewhere in Europe. He had by this time, and against ardent advice which predictably failed to stem the aspirations of his hubris, conceived his monumental and fateful scheme to invade Russia. On the 24th of June, the enormous French host, which tellingly now included 30,000 men he had taken from the campaign in Iberia, crossed the Niemen.

The Battle of Smolensk was fought on the 16th of August, and the Russians doggedly retreated to stand again close by their capital at the Battle of Borodino on the 7th of September. The battle was a stalemate though the casualties on both sides were enormous, which in the case of the French was particularly significant for they were far from home and deep in the heartland of their enemy. The Russians once again retreated passing through Moscow, and, on the 16th of September, Napoleon slept in the

Kremlin palace, occupying a city which patriotic incendiaries forthwith transformed into a funeral pyre. As the emperor contemplated the price and value of his achievement in the heat of those flames, the patient Russian Army, as the winds of Autumn grew progressively more chill, awaited the perennial and familiar arrival of its most formidable ally.

CHAPTER FOURTEEN

The Advance from Cadiz to Seville, 1812

As Wellington was advancing into the heart of Spain, the defence of Cadiz continued. Whilst the city remained indisputably under siege, the denial of its harbour to the French meant that Cadiz was also making a positive contribution to the war effort, since it remained a viable entry point in southern Spain for both men and materiel to move directly into Andalusia. The French were compelled, therefore, to commit resources to the region, remaining on the alert for sudden developments at hand which also prevented them from sending reinforcements to Joseph in Madrid. On the 16th of May, 1812, the town was subjected to a serious bombardment from thirty French gunboats in the Trocadero canal. This bombardment against the town and shipping was repeated on the 4th of July, but attention to the siege for a moment became less of a priority for Soult, by the landing of troops from English vessels farther to the east on the coast of Grenada.

No change, however, took place in the respective positions of the besieged and besiegers at Cadiz until August, when, the bombardment became serious and opposition to British influence within the walls increased from all quarters. However, these matters would, before long, become irrelevant for the victory of Salamanca in July, and the subsequent occupation of Madrid by the British Army, shook French confidence, and made it necessary for Joseph, if he wished to save the throne of his new kingdom, to concentrate his armies of the North and South. Joseph, after retreating into Valencia, sent Soult orders to come with all his forces to the assistance of the Army of the Centre for the recovery of Madrid. Wellington sent orders, at more or less the same time, to General Cooke to make a direct attack upon the French lines round Cadiz.

Prior to these last orders having been received, Colonel Skerrett, who had held Tarifa, had been ordered to embark at Cadiz with 4,000 troops, and land on the coast to the north. Six companies of the Third Battalion, First Guards, under Colonel Peregrine Maitland, who was appointed second in command, formed part of this expedition. The detachment of Guards accordingly marched on the morning of the 9th of August from their old quarters on the Isla de Leon to Cadiz and embarked the same day. On the following morning the expedition sailed for Huelva, on the coast, seventy miles to the north-west, arriving there in the middle of the night of the 11th.

Saltoun was of course, serving with this battalion in Cadiz and so took part in this joint expedition under the Spanish General Cruz Mourgeon and Colonel Skerrett which occurred in conjunction with Wellington's movements in central Spain, and with the eventual intention of joining with Hill's division, which was operating to the south of Wellington's advance upon Madrid. During the day the troops were put into boats, and after thirty-six cramped hours spent in them, the Guards were landed at Huelva on the night of the 13th whilst the rest of the army and its stores were landed on the 14th and 15th. The British element consisted of the Guards, the 87th and the 20th Portuguese Regiments amounting to 800 men. The Spanish force added a further 600 troops.

On the 16th the troops began their march up the country towards Seville, threatening the French lines of communications round Cadiz on their way, and, after halting that night at Trigeras, moved on the following day, to Niebla. Skerrett expected to make contact with the French in Niebla which was supposedly occupied by the enemy, but the place was discovered to be deserted. So, he continued his march on the 18th and 19th through Palma to Manzanilla, where the troops rested until the 24th. From Manzanilla a detachment of the Guards and others were despatched at eleven at night with instructions to attack the enemy known to be at St. Lucar la Major, near Seville (this enemy force was estimated to be about 350 cavalry and 200 infantry) and this assault was carried out successfully, driving in its outposts and pushing the enemy, 'through the streets with precipitation leaving some killed, wounded and prisoners', to quote Skerrett's report, without any loss to the attackers.

Soult by this point had no alternative but to abandon the siege of Cadiz, and on the 25th of August, after destroying the immense works at Chiclana and the Trocadero, as well as many guns, and a vast amount of stores, he retired, moving off in the direction of Seville. The blockade by land, which had lasted upwards of two and a half years, was finally at an end.

Skerrett's corps meanwhile, including the six companies of the Third Battalion, First Guards, under Maitland, preceded by the light company of the Guards, under Colonel Colquitt, with some hussars of the King's German Legion, marched all the night of the 25th from San Lucar, and reached the heights to the north of Seville on the following morning. They came in contact with the advanced posts of the enemy about three miles from Seville, drove them in, and about seven in the morning (Skerrett's report says it was the 27th) moved to the attack of the city. Seville is situated on the south bank of the Guadalquivir, and the allies approached it from the north, through the suburbs of Triana.

The Spanish element was directed to turn these suburbs on the right flank, while the British and Portuguese attacked in front. The British column advanced for more than two miles at the 'double-quick' and were, at the point of the bayonet, just in time to drive the French from the defence of a principal gateway and bridge of Triana as they were attempting to destroy it. As soon as the Spanish column had reached its appointed objective, the British cavalry and artillery advanced at a gallop, followed by the grenadiers of the Guards with the remainder of the infantry bringing up the rear. The bridge was damaged, but not sufficiently so to prevent the grenadiers of the Guards, preceded by the Spanish troops, who led the column, from passing over it. For a moment the attackers were checked by a heavy fire of musketry and grape in the streets, but they renewed the advance driving everything before them. Meanwhile volleys from the flanking columns made the enemy's position on the other side of the river untenable. The enemy's forces, which consisted of eight battalions and two regiments of cavalry, retired hastily and disorganised down the road to Cordoba, leaving behind them 200 prisoners together with all their baggage and valuables.

Colonel Skerrett's despatch stated:

> The conduct of every officer and soldier has been above praise. Where all have behaved well it is difficult to distinguish. I must, however, mention the detachment of the King's German Legion, commanded by Cornet Wiebolt; the artillery, by Captain Roberts; the detachment of the 95th, by Captain Cadoux, and the grenadiers of the First Regiment of Guards, by Captain Thomas. To Colonel Maitland, First Guards (second in command), I am much indebted, from the commencement of this service; and in the attack of Seville his military talents, intrepidity, and zeal were particularly conspicuous. I am also much indebted to Lieutenant-Colonel Colquitt, commanding a detachment of the First Regiment of Guards.

The captain of Rifles, Daniel Cadoux became famous in the annals of the 95th for his intrepid defence of a bridge across the Bidassoa in 1813 known as 'The Combat of Vera', when a company of seventy riflemen under his command held off Clausel's escaping rearguard under General of Division, Vandermaesen. Realising he was vastly outnumbered Cadoux called for support, but this was denied and he was ordered to retire. He ignored this order, fighting on doggedly until attrition wore down his little command. Vandermaesen and Cadoux both lay dead at the close of the action and the officer, by this point a major-general, who failed to support him was the same man who had once sung his

135

praises at Seville. Skerrett was replaced by Colborne and whilst commanding a brigade during the assault on Bergen-op-zoom in 1814 he was killed in action.

Saltoun kept a diary of this period which has survived and his own annotations of his experiences during the month of August 1812, obviously echo the historical record, but carry an immediacy of personal experience:

> *24th.*—Marched with a detachment at eleven at night, and attacked the enemy's outposts at San Lucar le Major, and drove them in with little loss on their side, and none on ours; distance four leagues.
>
> *25th.*—Fell back one league; took post near a river in the rear of San Lucar.
>
> *26th.*—Marched at five in the morning with the hussars to make a reconnaissance; the troops joined us next morning.
>
> *27th.*—Marched with the whole of the force towards Seville, fell in with the enemy at his advanced posts at Castellega, one league from Seville, drove them in, and about seven in the morning advanced to the attack of that place; distance of march four and a half leagues. The British column advanced for more than two miles at double-quick, and were just in time to drive the enemy from the bridge with the bayonet, as they were trying to cut it; at ten we were in complete possession of the place. The French force was eight battalions of infantry and two regiments of cavalry, commanded by Victor; ours consisted of 3500 Spaniards under Cruz Mourgeon, and 1500 British, with three six-pounders, under Colonel Skerrett, and the place was only carried by the rapidity of the British advance, which terrified the enemy.

The remaining four companies of the Third Battalion, First Guards, under Colonel Lambert, left the Isla on the 1st of September marching by a direct route for Seville though halting at Xeres, a few miles from Cadiz, until the 6th, as they waited for the infantry brigade under Lord Proby to join them. On the 7th, after a twenty-seven mile march over level country, but under a punishing burning sun, the command arrived at Utrera,

Battle of Seville

a day's march from Seville, where, on the 11th, the four companies were joined by the six companies of the battalion that had entered Seville on the 27th of the previous month.

These six companies, after halting four days in Seville, marched to nearby Alcala, where they remained till the 7th of September, when they moved for two days to Mayrena, returning on the 9th to Alcala, and on the 11th, after another short march, they joined their other four companies at Utrera. While the Third Battalion, First Guards remained in this town, the riflemen of the 95th and part of the artillery were stationed at Alcala, and the cavalry, the 47th and 87th British, and 20th Portuguese Regiments, and a brigade of guns remained at Headquarters in Seville. Colonel Colquitt, who had been severely wounded at Barrosa, unfortunately died of a fever brought on by fatigue while the battalion was at Utrera.

After a week's halt, the battalion received orders to join Wellington's army in the north of Spain so it moved to Seville on the 19th, and after again halting some days, Skerrett's brigade began its march on the 30th for Truxillo, passing Los Santos, Villafranca, Guarema, and Medellin. On the 11th of October they halted at Mayados, and next day at Truxillo, arriving at Talavera by Almarez on the 18th of October.

CHAPTER FIFTEEN

The Siege of Burgos and the Retreat, 1812

Wellington's talents, in many respects, epitomised the definition of military expertise of his time. Perhaps most importantly, like Marlborough, he was often able to prevail irrespective of the obstacles and difficulties with which he had to contend. These obstacles would include the limitations of his own resources of every kind to the behaviour of his unreliable allies, as well as the unambiguous intentions of his enemies. In the field, when able to manoeuvre, his efforts, supported by his brilliant little army 'that could go anywhere and do anything', were invariably met with qualified success if not, in every case, with an outright victory. It was well that Wellington possessed military genius, for he was invariably outnumbered in the Peninsula which made it essential that he chose his engagements with care, for his lines of communication and supply were long and he could not afford a contest of attrition.

The reduction of walled towns and citadels in this campaign was necessary, but these were perpetually problematic for the British Army. An assault required a concentration of suitable artillery, facilitated by a sizeable train and the skills of engineers, (all of which were in very short supply) and a commitment to the expenditure of seasoned troops that Wellington knew he could ill afford to lose for they were not readily or reliably replaceable.

Ciudad Rodrigo and Badajoz had both been bloody examples of the cost of assaults on formidable defensive works and by mid-September,1812, the fortifications of Burgos now stood in Wellington's way, for he believed it must be captured before he might safely pursue the French into Alava or Navarre. Furthermore, the decisive outcomes of his most recent successes meant that the French armies had consolidated into two dangerous masses. Soult, Suchet and Joseph had between them in excess of 130,000 men available for deployment. Once again, Wellington had to face the reality that with approximately 60,000 men as his disposal he could not afford to face such overwhelming numbers were they, or even a superior portion of them, sent in his direction.

The siege of Burgos lasted just one month from September 19th to October the 19th and was according to the historian, Professor Charles Oman, 'the most unfortunate operation he (Wellington) ever conducted'. Burgos, though small, was deceptively strong, whereas the materiel and personnel, as Wellington well knew, that could be brought for the attack was insufficient for the task, most especially in a dearth of heavy artillery. The transport needed to bring guns and their ammunition to the front was in particular short supply. Nevertheless, the assault commenced, but though some of the outer works were taken, four attempts to storm the castle failed. To their credit, the French made a determined defence of the place which resulted in time wasted for the British force (which was of necessity stationary), but which was time well spent in reorganisation and concentration elsewhere in preparation for an advance by the enemy.

Accordingly, King Joseph and Soult's forces, marched with 60,000 men on Madrid and towards Hill's inferior detached command, from the direction of Murcia, in the south-east, while simultaneously Souham was marching to relieve Burgos, at the head of a host comprised of the Armies of Portugal and the North. Wellington may well have been persuaded to fight Souham, were it not for the certainty of Hill's destruction by Soult.

The impossibility of that option meant it was imperative that the British Army be reunited at the earliest opportunity.

The retreat from Burgos had commenced on the 22nd of October; on the 24th the army halted behind the confluence of the Carrion and Pisuerga Rivers, and while in this position, the First Battalion, First Guards, under the command of Colonel M. C. Darby Griffith, joined it from England.

★★★★★★

The first battalion had returned home after the Walcheren campaign, in 1809, and on the 7th of September, 1812, it marched to Portsmouth, embarking on the 13th aboard the *Alfred* man-of-war, bound for Corunna, where after an easy passage it disembarked on the 26th of the same month. It had been originally planned, after the raising of the blockade, that the Third Battalion, First Guards should sail to Lisbon, with the other troops that had been employed in the defence of Cadiz. Having arrived it would be brigaded with the first battalion which would arrive, also at Lisbon, from England. However, as described, Wellington subsequently ordered the third battalion to depart Cadiz by land and join the army in the field, and in consequence the first battalion was sent to Corunna as its point of entry into the theatre. The 91st Regiment, 950 strong, was to be temporarily brigaded with it, and placed under Lord Dalhousie, while a draft of 250 men for the several battalions of Guards already in the Peninsula was to accompany the expedition.

Wellington wrote to Lieutenant-Colonel Bourke, on the 21st of September:—

> Sir,
>
> I wish the First Battalion, First Foot Guards to move through Gallicia, as already arranged; but, instead of turning off from the high road at Villa Franca, as directed when the enemy was in possession of Astorga, and it was supposed they would maintain that position, I wish them now to proceed to Astorga on to Benavente.
>
> Mr. White must make provision for them till they will arrive at Benavente. At Benavente, or before they will arrive there, a staff officer of this army shall meet them, and they will receive

further orders for their march.

The messenger who takes this has a letter from the quartermaster-general, for the commanding officer of the First Battalion, First Foot Guards, of which I enclose a duplicate, in case there is any mistake about that with which he is charged.

We took by storm on the 19th the outwork of the Castle of Burgos, with some loss.

I have, &c.,

Wellington.

The First Battalion, First Guards having landed at Corunna, marched by wings on the 30th of September, crossing over the battlefield which was painfully familiar to many still in the ranks. It halted at Lugo on the 5th and 6th of October, and was at Astorga on the 16th. The castle there had been destroyed and much of the town levelled with the ground including the chapter-house which lay in ruins. The cathedral had also been severely damaged. On the 19th the column reached Benavente, which had shared much the same kind of destruction. The battalion arrived at Ampadia, on the 23rd of October and on the following morning it was on the march for Palencia, at which time the commanding officer learned that Wellington was retreating from Burgos, and that the enemy was in close pursuit.

★★★★★★

Following the line of the canal to Duenas, the battalion eventually joined the main body of the British Army, where it bivouacked, with the rest of the division of Guards, on the right of the line. No sooner had the first battalion joined the main army, than it came in contact with the French. On the following morning, now part of the First Division, the battalion marched to the left to support the Fifth Division, who were engaging the enemy as it attempted to cross the Pisuerga River.

On the following day, the 26th, the retreat was continued towards Valladolid, the First Division halted at Cabeson. On reaching Valladolid, on the 29th, the news arrived that the French had crossed the river at Tordesillas, whereupon the First Division was sent to oppose them. Wellington had intended to await the arrival of Hill's corps, in a strong position, between Tordesillas and Rueda, but on the 6th of November the army fell back again to San Christoval, seven miles north of Salamanca. The First Division moved to Villares de la Reyna, within three miles of the city.

★★★★★★

While these events were in progress, Skerrett's little army, including the Third Battalion, First Guards, moved from Talavera de la Reyna on the 19th of October, and marching due east by Toledo, reached Puente Largo near Aranjuez on the 26th, where it fell in with Hill's corps, which, since the Battle of Salamanca, had been occupied in opposing the return of King Joseph and Soult to Madrid. The Guards were removed from Skerrett's command, and attached to the Fourth Division, under Cole, forming part of Hill's corps.

The notes from Saltoun's journal reveal that this junction had barely taken effect before the enemy made its appearance and fighting ensued

26th.—To the park at Aranjuez, four leagues, there had been an alarm during the night, and General Hill had ordered the bridge to be destroyed. Bivouacked. The park very fine; a number of trees planted in avenues, but marshy.

27th.—Halt; the enemy made his appearance in front of Aranjuez.

28th.—The enemy occupied the town and gardens of the palace, on the opposite side of the Tagus.

29th.—Retired at one in the morning over the Jarama River, and took post on the Madrid road, in rear of the Puente Larga, which we were preparing to destroy. In the evening marched to Cien Pozuelos, one league.

30th.—The enemy attacked Puente Larga, the mine of which failed, and were repulsed with loss by the 47th regiment.

Joined headquarters as orderly officer.

The historical record of this period corresponds with Saltoun's brief notes. In consequence of the raising of the siege of Burgos, Hill was now, by order of Wellington, making preparations for a retreat from the advanced position he had occupied, and the outposts of the Fourth Division (which was selected as his rear guard) were, on the 27th of October, engaged with Soult's advance on the Jarama. Hill decided, in order to protect his retreat towards Wellington's army, to blow up the bridge across the Tagus at Puente Largo, and the Third Battalion, First Guards was tasked to cover this operation by holding any interference by the enemy in check. The engineering work, as usual owing to a lack of equipment, progressed slowly and on the 29th the third battalion was relieved by Skerrett's brigade, consisting of the 47th and 87th Regiments, and marched to Cien Pozeulos (Ciempozuelos), south of Madrid.

On the 30th the enemy attacked in force, and the attempt to blow up the bridge having failed, the French tried to carry it at the point of the bayonet, but were vigorously repulsed by the 47th Regiment. However, Nature was about to break the impasse in the favour of the French in ways no one could forecast.

Over the next twelve hours, a sudden fall of four feet in the depth the River Tagus made the fords across it once again practicable to effect a crossing without reliance on the bridge and the British position became untenable. The division continued its retreat without delay, marching all night towards Madrid and halting outside the city.

On the 1st of November, General Hill destroyed his stores and blew up the Retiro palace which had been put to use as barracks and an arsenal, and on the same day, the Third Battalion, First Guards, still forming part of Cole's rear guard, marched through Madrid, and halted on the 2nd at Alvara. The French Army entered Madrid as soon as it was evacuated.

Saltoun accompanied Hill's headquarters to Aravaca, and to the Escurial, on the 4th. The battalion crossed the Guadarama mountains, and onwards through the province of Old Castille, and across the Tormes River, to Espinar, Lavajos, and Villa Nueva de Gomez, where on the 5th November Saltoun rejoined his battalion, which retired to the heights of San Christoval, in the vicinity of Salamanca, on the 9th November, just one day after

Wellington with his army had reached them.

Saltoun noted in his journal the astonishing distance he and his men had travelled since coming ashore from the boats at Huelva.

> *9th.*—Marched in the afternoon to Salamanca, and were quartered in a convent. The first time we had been under cover, except at Cien Pozuelos, since we left Añover on the 26th October. Distance marched from Huelva 636 miles. Joined Lord Wellington's army, which had retired here from Burgos.
> With Wellington's army the battalion retreated through Ciudad Rodrigo, Gallegos, and past Fuentes d'Onoro, until the 8th of December, when the troops went into cantonments, and the Guards were quartered in Viseu, Mondeo, and Spraida. Had at this place marched from Huelva 800 miles, computing the Spanish league at four English miles.

On the 11th, the third battalion went into cantonments at Aldea Seco, about three miles from Salamanca, having marched 640 miles from Seville, and here the first and third battalions of the First Guards again met and were brigaded together. The Brigade of First Guards, and the Second Brigade, consisting of the first battalions of the Coldstream and Third Regiments, was now formed into a division.

Major-General H. F. Campbell, of the First Guards, who had formerly commanded the Second Brigade, was promoted to a Division, and Colonel Hon. T. Fermor of the Third Regiment, was placed in temporary command of it until Major-General Hon. Ed. Stopford, also of the Third Guards, could take over. Major-General G. Cooke, of the First Guards, had been ordered to remain for a time at Cadiz. Major-General William Wheatley, who had commanded a portion of the Guards at the battle of Barrosa, died at the Escurial on the 1st of September and the command of the First Brigade of Guards, (first and third battalions First Guards) went to Major-General K. A. Howard, of the Coldstreams.

The united British Army now mustered an impressive 64,000 men and seventy pieces of artillery, but it was pursued by the combined three French corps with in excess of 95,000 men with 120 guns. During the whole war the French had never before gathered so large a force upon a single line and it presented an intimidating prospect. Wellington turned at bay momentarily on the night of the 13th to 14th of November. The Brigade of First Guards, and the rest of the First Division, under Sir Edward Paget, took up a position on the Arapiles, near Aldea Tejada, to secure the passage over the Zurgain, but nothing came of it.

Soult, however, pressed on, always turning the allied right, passing three divisions over the Tormes, and threatening the allied communications. Wellington, after destroying his stores and banking on the inability of his pursuers to maintain the chase for much longer, retreated further to Valmuya.

On the 17th the First Division halted at San Munos, on the Huebra, where to the relief of all concerned, the active pursuit of the French ceased from 'a dearth of provisions and the effects of miserable weather'. The French also were, in fact, in a desperate state of exhaustion, and were in no better condition than their quarry. On the 18th the fugitives marched on by very bad roads to San Spiritus. On the 19th they arrived at Ciudad Rodrigo and on the 20th, the First Guards, passed through it, crossing the Agueda. The first battalion was then cantoned at Carpes, and the third battalion, after an arduous march, arrived at Gallegos, near the Portuguese frontier.

This retreat from Salamanca, though it has been given far less retrospective consideration, bore more than passing similarities to Moore's retreat to Corunna, for its demands had been very severe, and the army was utterly exhausted. The weather had now broken as the winter months progressed, the rain fell in torrents and thick mists regularly obscured the way. The column churned the ground into a quagmire so that the troops could hardly move as the roads were transformed to ribbons of mud.

Saltoun wrote in a letter home an anecdote of this period which, with the benefit of retrospection, has an element of humour to it which was probably absent at the time these events occurred and to those who were involved in it.

The British Army on the march in Spain by Thomas Rowlandson

When on a march, I generally carried a large and strong umbrella. It served for a walking-stick, and as I had coated it with oil varnish, it was waterproof, and many a wetting it saved me. Upon one occasion, however, it took revenge for all its previous benefits. We had halted after dark in ploughed land, on the steep slope of a hill, and tired as we all were, it was impossible in the dark to attempt to better our position. The men settled themselves to rest as best they could. It was raining heavily, and blowing hard; but, fortunately, the drift was down the slope of the hill, and I therefore sat down, with the umbrella over my shoulders, to pass the night.

A brother officer sat down between my knees, and another took a similar position between his knees, all three more or less sheltered by the umbrella. After moodily chatting a while we dropped off to sleep, but how long we slept I cannot say, I only know that I was suddenly roused by the most unpleasant hip bath I ever got: the rain water descending the hill side had been dammed up in the furrow, above where we sat, by the edge of the umbrella resting on the ground; some movement of mine, in my sleep, must have raised it, and the water rushed down upon us, drenching me and the one next to me up to the waist, but our friend below did not escape even so well; in his sleep he lay down, and the rush of water took him in the nape of the neck, and went right through him from head to foot. Three such miserable wretches, as we were till morning broke, were never seen.

The soldiers of the rank and file, as usual, fared poorly on the retreat for they were frequently under arms for long periods without rations. So hard pressed were they, that meat, when it was available at all, was eaten half-cooked from the embers of their camp-fires and, at times when no provisions were brought up at all, they were reduced to eating boiled acorns as a substitute for bread.

In the field, British soldiers of the time had demonstrated that they were incapable, in extreme circumstances, of self-control or collective responsibility and for that they cannot be blamed, for the ruling classes (which embraced many officers of the army) had, in the main, little faith in them and believed that the only way to control the lower orders was to hold them strictly in check by the disciplines of fear of punishment.

The British oligarchy, in turn, were fearful of the power of the masses for they had seen mobs of the disaffected running riot at home in recent years. Rebellions of disaffection in Scotland were still considered probable and garrisons were positioned to repress them should they arise, whilst affairs in Ireland were in seemingly perpetual foment. These anxieties became more acute within the age of revolutions which appealed to the oppressed, especially as the fruit of that tree was Napoleon's army. Parliamentary reform demonstrations which occurred in England in 1819 resulted in civilian deaths and reinforced all prejudices including, no doubt, those of the Duke of Wellington.

During hard retreats or costly assaults when the leash of discipline was loosened or irrevocably lost, the 'dangerous and unruly beast' was bound to shake itself free, for the army had no solution to restrain it before the fact. There was, furthermore, no institutional will to countenance systems to foster self-reliance and initiative, nor were measures instituted which would avert dire consequences when order was tested to a potential breaking point. That initiative was needed for most (if not all) the regiments of the army, as was the creation of effectively functioning essential support services. Both would come about much later, but in the meantime those who could readily understand that the way to improve a horse was not to neglect it then beat it ever more severely, could not countenance that the same principle could be applied to a man.

So inevitably, as the conditions of the retreat from Burgos worsened there came a point when discipline broke down and straggling became ever more prevalent. Hundreds of sick and exhausted men were left behind to perish or to fall into the hands of the French, whose inclinations to be merciful were inconsistent. At the point that men concluded they must ensure their own personal survival, all the constraints that bound them were abandoned to the necessities of the moment and so rapacity, marauding, and the usual degradations ensued. Wellington issued severe orders to recover discipline and a memorandum of censure, attributing the rank and file's conduct to the inattention of their officers, though he had been as impotent as had Moore to avert an issue he knew was certain to arise. He never received an epiphany on the matter to the end of his days, for he was no reformer. In fact, these kinds of occurrences only confirmed Wellington's reactionary convictions, though to be fair to him, once the army was in the field *sans* reform the die was cast.

The soldiers of the Third Battalion, First Guards had the advantages of veteran campaigners, having spent an extended period in the field, and were in a fine state of discipline to cope with the hardships that came their way. Since leaving Cadiz, on the 20th of August, the men had been constantly on the march, a distance of 650 miles. The problems arising from a breakdown of order which beset the army did not generally apply to the Guards or to the Light Division. It had been so during Moore's retreat and so it was again on the retreat from Burgos and these exceptions were, as a matter of record, not a surprise to Wellington. One may speculate that these troops, who suffered equally with no preferential treatment, had the greatest sense of their own identities creating an *esprit de corps* and self-worth which positively influenced their behaviour. Perversely, the fine examples of these paragons served as a double-edged sword as regarded addressing or ignoring the fundamental issues that beset the army.

CHAPTER SIXTEEN

The Decline of the Empire of the French, 1812

Despite the ostensibly disappointing end to the campaign, the net results of the year 1812 for the allied cause in the Peninsula for Wellington and his army were most satisfactory. Professor Charles Oman summarised it thus, 'Though the French had reoccupied Madrid and Toledo, they had been compelled to evacuate all of southern Spain. Estremadura, Andalusia and La Mancha had been completely freed from the invaders; and the casualties inflicted upon the imperial armies had exceeded 40,000 men. They were now thrown upon the defensive and had lost confidence in their ultimate success.'

Nor was the situation in Iberia the limit of Napoleon's problems. His vainglorious campaign to invade and humiliate Russia and its monarch had been over reaching in its aspirations and had gone disastrously awry. The emperor, in the early part of October, recognising that he had over played his hand and that he had brought his army very far from friendly territory was trying to induce Emperor Alexander to open negotiations which would lead towards an unchallenged withdrawal, but no reply was given to his proposals. The Russian Army knew that time was on its side and was waiting to fall upon the forlorn French with all its forces, as soon as they should begin to retreat.

As winter approached Napoleon left the Kremlin in Moscow on the 20th of October with 100,000 men and 600 guns. A battle was fought at Milo Jaroslovitz, in which the French remained masters of a ruined town, but still threatened on both flanks, they were forced to continue their retreat. By November the Russian winter set in with its usual vengeance, snow fell to blanket the landscape, winds howled through the forests and temperatures plummeted. The French Army staggered westward, poorly clothed, short of provisions, rarely able to find shelter and all the while the Russians gnawed at the enormous, but ever depleting column like wolves upon the trail of a herd.

The emperor was at Smolensk in early November and, with the Old Guard, quitted it by the middle of the month. He left the remains of his army at Smorgoni early in December, and, travelling night and day, arrived in Paris on the 19th of the month. When the French rearguard left Russian soil on the 14th of December, the army which had marched towards Moscow some 685,000 strong had, according to legend, been reduced to just 22,000 bedraggled survivors Allowing for considerable disparity of opinion on that matter and even discounting the multitude of civilian camp followers who had perished along the way, it was indisputable that the magnificent *Grande Armée* that had marched to the east under its eagles had effectively ceased to exist.

★★★★★★

After remaining for eight days at Gallegos, close to Ciudad Rodrigo, Wellington's army continued its retreat towards Portugal, and the First Brigade of Guards, marching on the 28th to San Pedro and Val de la Mula, and passing the site of the Battle of Fuentes d'Onoro, eventually crossed the frontier.

Saltoun in a letter to his mother of the 26th December, wrote that the likelihood of his return to England to take his seat in the House of Lords as one of the Representative Peers of Scotland depended upon whether military operations would begin early in the following year or not.

On Sunday, the 29th December, the Third Battalion, First Guards was quartered at Medo, and the first battalion, after crossing the River Coa, reached Castello del Mendo. Thereafter, the two battalions advanced by easy marches to Lamegal, Alverea, Francesco, Aguiar de Beira, through Asamel, Villa Formosa, and Tugal; and finally, on the 8th of December marched into winter cantonments. The first battalion took up residence in Viseu and the third battalion was allocated to Mondao, Spraida de Rondio, and adjacent villages.

Here the brigades, after their recent sufferings and hardships, were able to enjoy a period of rest from their labours. Saltoun had come to the end of six years of soldiering with the First Guards against Napoleon's French Army and on reflection it had not been a period that had involved him in much military success, for he had taken part in two terrible retreats, a disastrous blunder of a campaign in the Low Countries and had been in-carcerated behind the walls of besieged Cadiz for months. Whilst his regiment had the battle honour of 'Barrosa' to its credit he had missed the battle, for he was with the third battalion in Lon-don. Nevertheless, the tone of his communications was never less than confident, positive and animated. He wrote a letter to his mother during this rest period on the 10th of January, 1813.

Nel Spraida, Portugal.
10th January

My Dear Mother,

I have no news, and very little to write about, but as Tuesday is our post-day for England, I just send you a few lines to say we are all going on well, and as comfortable as we can expect to be. Lord Wellington is daily looked for from Cadiz, and when he arrives, we shall probably take the field, or soon after, as our pressing the enemy here will keep up the spirit in Russia more than anything else, should Napoleon determine to try another campaign in the north. Besides there is no reason why our cav-alry should not eat the green forage in Castille, instead of the enemy's, as by this means the harvest in this country will be saved to the people, which otherwise must be consumed when green by our cavalry, should we remain in our present canton-ments.

I do not think I shall go to England if I can avoid it. In the first place, I cannot stay with you more than three or four days consistently with my own opinions as a military man; moreover, as I must travel with the greatest expedition, it will cost me between two and three hundred, which I have many other ways of disposing of, although none that would give me so much satisfaction.

Macdonald is here, and begs to be kindly remembered to you. He wishes you would do him a favour, which is to thank Mrs. Montgomery in his name for the music which she sent him. I do not know if you are acquainted with her, but she is the mother of the Miss Montgomerys who dance French country dances.

It is at present a hard frost, and we have turned one of our landlord's windows in the principal *Sala* into an excellent fireplace, to the great annoyance of the landlady; however, when we are gone she may return it into a window, and the *Sala*, which in our opinion is much improved by it, will not then have suffered in hers, and it is easily done, for glass is not a necessary article to a window in this country.

If any friend is coming out to join the regiment, pray send me some snuff; but it is no use sending it to Lisbon, as it is as difficult to get anything from thence to the army on a private account as it would be in England to transport Somerset House all standing to Aberdeen.

> Love to William (*his brother*) and the girls.
> Your dutiful son,
>
> Saltoun.

The First Division of the British Army now consisted of the First Brigade of Guards, under Major-General Howard and the Second Brigade of Guards, under Major-General Hon. E. Stopford. Also included were two other brigades, consisting of the first, second, and fifth battalions of King's German Legion, under Major-General Lowe and first and second King's Light German Legion, under Colonel Halket, all under Lieutenant-General Hon. Sir William Stewart. Captain Carey le Marchant, of the First Guards, (eldest son of John Le Marchant, one of the finest cavalry commanders of his day, who was killed at Salamanca the previous year) was appointed *Aide-de-Camp* to the Lieutenant-General. Carey Le Marchant was seriously wounded at San Sebastian and died at St. Jean de Luz shortly afterwards.

The First Brigade of Guards had not been long in their winter quarters before the reaction from hard work to repose produced widespread sickness, and a low fever broke out amongst the men. Within a few days of their arrival at Carpes and Gallegos, nearly 700 men were declared sick out of a total of 2,541 men, while there were only 176 effective reinforcements available attached to the second battalion in England to make up the shortfall. Shocking though this was, the Guards fared better than the army taken as a whole wherein 18,000 men were sick to 31,000 effective, or about two to three, while one regiment had above 700 sick and 500 effective.

The light companies of the First Guards presented a very great contrast in health to the rest of the army. The light company of the third battalion, which included Saltoun, quartered in advance at Spraida, covering the rest of the army since the 12th of January, had retained its health and at the beginning of February had only eight men on the sick list. Sickness, however, generally persisted throughout the winter months and only partially improved by the warmer weather of approaching Spring so the battalions of Guards were, on the 18th of February, removed to the neighbouring villages in the hope that they might become healthier. The change of scene did nothing to improve the situation, so at last they were ordered to Oporto, about sixty miles away on the coast, in the hopes that the sea air might bring the troops back to health.

On the 8th of February Saltoun once again wrote to his family and within his letter, perhaps inevitably, made reference to his concerns about the sickness which had struck the Brigade of Guards. Interestingly, in the same letter, he passed comment on the criticisms Wellington had made about the conduct of the army during the retreat from Burgos and Salamanca. It is quite apparent that Saltoun was very annoyed at Wellington's high-handed allocation of blame to regimental officers and that Saltoun believed, with some justification perhaps, that responsibility ultimately lay with the person in the position of most authority. It is clear that Saltoun understood that the key to the maintenance of order lay in ensuring that the basic needs of the troops in the logistics of provisions, elementary requirements of subsistence and transportation for the sick and wounded were available and maintained at all times.

I am very sorry, but not surprised, at a certain letter having crossed the Atlantic; it should never have gone beyond the orderly books of the army, . . . and it is foolish for a general to abuse his army for disorders arising from the want of a proper commissariat, which Frederic the Great says it is his first duty to provide.

It is no excuse for him that there is no wood in a country, but it is a very great one for a soldier pulling down a house to cook his provisions with the materials; and in everything, when one disorder is permitted, another will soon creep in upon the heels of it.

I do not mean to say that the army was not in a very bad state, but every man knows, who has ever seen an army, that such must be the case, if that army be ill supplied with bread; and the saddle should always be put on the right horse.

To say nothing of the hardships of the first part of the retreat, which were tolerably severe, the commissary might, and ought to have been at San Muños with a supply of bread for the army; we should then have had ample means of carrying the wounded and those men who were unable to march from fatigue, and their number would also have been very much lessened by the seasonable arrival of the bread, which would have enabled many to go through the very severe march we had from that place, for an extra half pound of over-driven beef is a very poor substitute for a pound and a half of bread, especially when that is issued for three days running.

Saltoun, in common with many other good officers, resented Wellington's censure. In measure, he felt the understandable sting of personal criticism with regard to the discharging of his duty in circumstances which he felt he could not control and secondly from the feeling that it was unjust to blame the soldiers for the disorder caused, in particular, by the failures of the commissariat. That Saltoun had a reasonable point there can be no doubt, but whether his suggested solution would have actually provided a remedy to all the army's ills under all of these kinds of circumstances remains moot for the societal influences that created the nature of the soldiers of Wellington's army were several and deep rooted.

Nevertheless, Saltoun had every reason to feel affection for and faith in his own guardsmen and this would have fundamentally informed his opinions. One cannot take the contents of the following extract from one of Saltoun's letters home as necessarily typical of the relationships between officers and their men of every regiment in the British Army of the period, but it does speak to the quality of the Guards of all ranks and underlines the veracity of the often quoted Biblical quotation from Galatians, 'Whatever a man soweth, so shall he reap'.

We had been marching (during the retreat) through difficult country, and on very bad roads, when, upon the halt for the night being ordered, we officers of the light company had the unwelcome intelligence conveyed to us that although the rations for the men had arrived all right, our mule, with all our supplies, had broken down some miles to the rear, and that we were in consequence supper-less.

As we were very hungry this was far from agreeable, and we sat down under a tree in no very cheery humour; but after a while were roused by the approach of the senior private of the company.

He carried a mess tin in each hand, which prevented him from saluting; but his words were very much to the point, 'Gentlemen, the men are very sorry to hear as how your mule has broke down and you ain't got no supper, so, says we, let's each give a little bit of our own, and it's in these here tins, and we hope you'll take it, gentlemen.'

Take it! we were only too glad to get it, and capital it was; but the circumstance showed what care soldiers will take of their officers if they like them, and I especially noticed that the oldest private was the spokesman, and that none of the non-commissioned officers were asked to interfere in what was an affair of kindly feeling, and not of duty.

The brigade broke up from its cantonments on the 26th and 27th of March, and on arrival at Oporto, on the 1st of April, occupied the St. Ovadio Barracks. The sick moved on the 7th by Lamego and Rego on the bank of the Douro, and down to Oporto. The numbers of men in hospital steadily decreased, but the effective strength of the First Brigade of Guards, was still very low, the first battalion having only 355 men, and the third battalion 430 men, fit for duty.

CHAPTER SEVENTEEN

The Remote Courtship of Lord Saltoun, 1813

Saltoun obtained a leave of absence and returned to England where, however, he remained only a few weeks before sailing on about the 11th of April from Falmouth to rejoin the army in Spain. However, this visit, though short in duration, proved to be one of the most important interludes of his life, as he then made the acquaintance of the lady who would become his future wife, Catharine, one of the three daughters of the late Lord Chancellor, Edward Thurlow, 1st Baron Thurlow, who had died in 1806 never having been married. The peculiar spelling of Catharine is confirmed as correct since it appears on Saltoun's letters to her.

As Saltoun was about to return to the peninsula he wrote a letter to Catharine Thurlow, and of course, in this correspondence quite another tone appears compared to the letters he had written to his family. It appears from the contents of this letter that the developing romance was an event that both Alexander and Catharine accepted was best kept a secret at that time (and for the foreseeable future) from Saltoun's mother, Lady Margery Saltoun, and we may readily speculate, given Saltoun's position and times, why that may have been the case.

His reference to Lady Lansdown(e) in this letter, probably concerned a ball or *soirée* to which he and Catharine Thurlow had both been invited. Their hostess would have been Lady Louisa Lansdowne, who was the wife of Lord Henry Petty

MARY AND CATHARINE THURLOW AS CHILDREN

who had been Chancellor of the Exchequer following Pitt, the younger. The simple fact was that Saltoun heartily disliked society occasions of this kind and often made excuses to avoid attending them.

Falmouth,
Friday night, 10 April 1813.

Dear Miss Thurlow,

Was ever anything in the world, my dear Miss Thurlow, half so provoking?

The mail has just this moment come in with an order to detain the packet till tomorrow, so that after all I might have remained in town another night, and gone to Lady Lansdown's; not that I myself had any wonderful inclination to wait on her Ladyship or the amiable Miss Giffard—for I could have passed the evening much more to my own satisfaction in Grosvenor Street— but you wished me to stay for it, and that is quite a sufficient reason for regretting I did not.

I believe the packet was detained in consequence of a dispatch, which I met between Bagshot and Egham, and which most probably brought some letters that it was necessary to answer immediately. I had a great mind to return when I found out that it was a dispatch from Falmouth; but as it might have been from America or any other place, as likely as from Spain—which I had then no means of ascertaining—I was obliged to proceed, doubting all the way, and now find that I might have returned without risk.

I have just written two long letters to her Ladyship (*his mother*) on business, and after sealing one of them, and just as I was going to send it to the post, I by accident looked at the seal. I had put more wax on than I generally do, and in pressing my own seal some of the wax had risen from the corner, and had taken the impression of your cipher so perfectly, that I thought her Ladyship had seen that seal so often that she must have known it again; at least I should anywhere. I thought it a lucky chance that had made me look at the seal, and with a dab of hot wax blotted it out. It will, however, make me more careful in future. This is a horrible dull place—nothing in the world to be seen except the surrounding country; but that I am well acquainted with, as I was here three weeks once. And moreover, it is horribly ugly. But I am telling a bit of a story, for I see they have got the invisible girl here, and I believe the actual one that we went to see in Leicester Fields. Do you remember that? It was before you left St. James' Square.

When I was here before, there was a play, a tolerable good set, but the waiter—who, by-the-by, is a Methodist, and a rank one—told me that a play-house was Satan's ground, and that the people of this town would not countenance such profane works. I told him they were a parcel of d— fools, but could not convert him for all that.

By this time, I dare say, you will be tired of reading, though in this instance, on my honour, I am not tired of writing, for I *must* think, and so it is easy work to write, even although it is nothing but nonsense, and shall not therefore venture to read it over. Pray tell me how Lady Lansdown's went off, and if my mother was there. If you write me, direct 1st Guards, 1st Division, British Army, Spain.

God bless you, my dear Miss Thurlow, and believe me ever yours,

Saltoun.

Saltoun's letter to Catharine Thurlow, written and posted immediately prior to his sailing for Portugal was followed by another written after his arrival in Lisbon. It is not difficult to appreciate how a young man with romance primarily on his mind would feel the compulsion to write more frequently than had been his habit. The tone and content of this letter is accordingly light-hearted and full of gossip intended to entertain his lady, as one might expect. The A.D.C or *aide-de-camp* referred to in the letter was James Hay, the son of William Hay, 17th Earl of Erroll.

He was an ensign in Saltoun's regiment and in 1813, just 16 years old and had lost his mother in the previous year. In this letter we discover he was acting the *beau* to a young lady at a society ball. He would also attend the Duchess of Richmond's famous ball in Brussels given before the Battle of Waterloo. The duchess's daughter, Georgiana later wrote that, 'he was a dashing, merry youth full of military ardour, delighted at the idea of going into action and all the honours he was to gain'. Tragically, however, he was shot and instantly killed as he rode at Saltoun's side in the battle at Quatre Bras.

Lisbon, Portugal,
1st May 1813.

My dear Miss Thurlow,

I have now, my dear Miss Thurlow, been here ten days, and am as heartily sick of the place as ever I was of anything in my life; it is certainly, take it altogether, the dirtiest town that ever a man got into.

Tomorrow I leave this to proceed to Oporto, where my regiment is now stationed, which place I shall reach on the 10th, and I understand we are likely to march from thence, in order to take the field, about the 12th, when the work for the year will begin.

I have been detained here waiting for some things that were left behind by my servant's negligence, and which came by the last packet. By the same conveyance I was given to understand that the A.D.C., Lord J. Hay, has had the supreme felicity of succeeding me in Mrs. B.'s good graces, and had the honour of starting Miss Di. at the second ball; but I strongly suspect, from the wording of said information, that poor I was again to have been brought forward, which would have been rather too much of a good thing, and too much, they say, is good for nothing. Had I remained, which—not on that account—I now regret I did not, I might, you know, have got tipsy and forgot it, or perhaps, indeed I may say more likely, Grosvenor Street might have seen me instead of Portman Square.

How fond the world is of manoeuvring, while we poor devils have not the credit of even the slightest penetration. Since I have been here, I have gone through the regular forms of the place, dined with all the great people, been to some routs and to one ball—a most Hottentot concern. Fancy a parcel of people, whom God never meant to be active, striving to dance Scotch reels, while the fiddlers were doing their best to play them as like waltzes as the music will admit of. I was obliged to perform in one not to seem fine, and that I thought was quite sufficient. They are certainly the most humdrum set I ever met with; very different from Spain, equally depraved, but do not carry it off so well.

This is opera night here as well as in London. I do not know if

163

you have been there; I, you see, have not, for by this time it must be over in both places; but I have been, if not more usefully, at least more agreeably employed. Since I have been quartered in an excellent house, and as accident would have it, it stands on the Monte de Santa Catherina, so you see my saint does not forget me even in this country.

I mean to go to Oporto by Cintra and Mafra, both which places are well worth seeing, and perhaps I may not again have such a good opportunity of going to them, and from time to time, if you do not prevent me, I shall give you an account of my peregrinations.

It is now very late, though I believe I have left you later; but as I have a long way to ride tomorrow, I must go and get some sleep: so goodnight, my dear Miss Thurlow, and believe me ever yours

S——

By the middle of the month of May, Saltoun had travelled as he had intended to Oporto to rejoin his regiment. As one may readily expect, Saltoun was still taken with his burgeoning romance with Catharine Thurlow and had received a letter from her to which he hastened a reply. The reader will discover the usual reports concerning pleasurable distractions, but the losses among the troops from sickness were demonstrably of concern to Saltoun and he makes reference to them within this letter. He also reported that although the army was taking to the field, the Guards were, for the time being to stay in Oporto.

Oporto, Portugal,
14 May 1813.

My dear Miss Thurlow,
Yours of the 20th April I received the morning after I wrote you. The packet came in during the night, and as I expected I should hear from you I was determined not to leave Lisbon till the letters were given out, and should have answered you sooner, but from the road that we came by not being the one of communication, I was obliged to wait till I came here, which I did yesterday; and as you assure me you will not tire of reading whenever I write, depend upon it there is nothing next to hearing from you that gives me so much pleasure as writing to you.

164

I was obliged to leave off writing to go and fire a salute in honour of the Prince Regent of Portugal, it being his birthday; but it is of no consequence, as I find this letter cannot go before Tuesday next, which is our post-day for England, and as this is Friday I shall at all events have time enough to finish it.

The general orders for the commencement of the campaign are arrived, and the divisions will march to their separate points in a few days. Lord Wellington has, however, determined not to move *us* for the present, and they say it will be a month before we begin our march.

We are certainly much better, and the men begin to look something like soldiers again, but it is shocking to think that since the month of December last we have buried eight hundred men out of two thousand, that is three hundred more than had died when I left the Brigade to go to England, but I am happy to say we have lost no men during the last three weeks, and those that are still in hospital are in a fair way of recovering; but, however, this is all Greek to you.

This is a fine large town, much cleaner and better in every respect than any place I have yet seen in Portugal, and the people have been very civil to the officers, and have given them a number of balls and other entertainments. We are to have a grand ball tonight, but I have not determined as yet whether I shall go to it or not; and if I am in the same mind after dinner that I am at present, I shall certainly not go to it, for just now I have not the slightest inclination. We have also a theatre where they act Portuguese plays, and I believe sometimes an opera, which last may be tolerable; but as to a play it must be but a very moderate performance, at least cannot have much to amuse an Englishman who does not understand ten words of the language.

And so you were disappointed in not hearing from me on the Monday after I left: I own you had hit the day off cleverly enough, and I had intended my letter to have been in town that morning; but although I knew that the mail-coach left Falmouth at three in the morning, I did not know that the post-office closed at ten at night, which was the reason you did not hear before Tuesday.

My tent and everything that had been left behind came to Lisbon a few days before I received your letter, and I have got them with me, and the only thing I now wish is that I may not be long without an opportunity of using them, for it is very provoking to be kept hanging on in this place when the army moves, as I could have passed the same time so much more to my satisfaction in England. You say it is not fair to trouble me with cross-writing; all I can say is that, as long as the writing is not cross, I do not care how much cross-writing there is: I shall not, however, give you any more of it at present, but leave what is not already crossed in case anything should happen before Tuesday.

Last night I went to the ball, which was really a very good one; two sets of about thirty couple each, and some tolerably pretty women. I find everybody here can speak French, and most of them English.

I have just got my papers from England, but no letters from home. I see your name mentioned as a dancer at the Miss Pritchards' ball in Green Street; was it you or your cousin? The people appear to be quite mad about Cossacks, and the Princess of Wales—certainly the people of England are, without any exception, the greatest fools in the world. I must own, however, I should like to see this Don Cossack myself, for if he is anything near the description of him, he must be a very fine fellow.

By this time, you must be heartily tired of deciphering this scrawl. I long to hear from you, and believe me I remain affectionately yours,

Saltoun.

P.S.—James Macdonald, whom you know, left this yesterday for England.

(This final note refers to the son of Lord Macdonald who was also an officer in the First Guards, killed at the disastrous assault on the French garrison at Bergen-op-Zoom in 1814.)

At the end of May, Major-General Howard, the brigadier, was promoted to the command of the First Division and Major-General John Lambert succeeded him in the command of the First Brigade of Guards. Major-General Disney, third major, continued in command of the Home District.

The main body of the army took the field towards the end of May. At that time the First Brigade of Guards were beginning to recover from the fatal sickness which had ravaged it and the men began again to look like soldiers. Since the month of December, the deaths had been averaging four or five per day. Given these severe losses it was decided to leave the brigade at Oporto some time longer. By the month of July, the First Guards had actually buried, since the beginning of the year, 800 out of 2,500 men.

In Saltoun's letter to Catharine Thurlow, sent in the middle of June he once again focused on the lighter aspects of his time in Portugal, but he also informed Catharine that he knew the time was approaching when the Guards would march to join the main army. In this estimation he was entirely correct, for nine days later on the 24th of June, the regiment received orders to take the field.

Oporto, Portugal,
15th June 1813.

My dear Miss Thurlow,

I did not write you by the last packet, for the post leaves this place on a Tuesday, and last Tuesday was the day before our grand ball which we gave the natives, and as I had been named as one of the committee for conducting the said ball, I had so much to do that I had not time to write.

It went off with great *éclat*, and, thank God, is now over, and what is not the worst part of it, *paid for.* You may guess the crush and trouble in this place—where there are no Mr. Gunters—in getting together the necessary apparatus for giving a hot supper to three hundred and fifty people, and the drill that was required previously to instruct the servants how to put the supper on the tables; but, however, we got them tolerably expert before the day, and it went off very well.

This place is just beginning to be hot, but I believe they never have any heat here equal to what it is to the south of Spain; however, I hope we shall not remain here to try.

We are now as strong as we shall be this year, and daily expect our order to march for the army, which is by this time near Valladolid; we had letters from it the day before yesterday. The 10th Hussars were engaged near Tordesillas, and defeated the 22nd and 23rd French Cavalry, with great loss on the part of the French. Ours was slight; one officer and seventeen men killed, and Captain Loyd wounded and taken, but left behind on his parole. This is the second time the cavalry have been engaged since the beginning of the campaign, and they have conducted themselves very gallantly on both occasions, which is a good thing, as last campaign they were rather in the background.

The principal lion here now is a man whose name, I believe, is Pearson, and he is a Pat, (*Irishman*) but he calls himself an Italian, and says his name is Personi. He certainly is a wonderful strong man. He walks about with ease to himself with seven men on him, and for his benefit, which takes place this week, he is to carry eleven; but the most singular thing that he does is, he puts a man on a cross, the pole of which is 12 feet long, and balances it on his chin. I confess I have no wish to be the man on the top of it.

I have this moment got a letter from Eleanor, (his sister), by which I find my mother is still at Brompton. She says you are well. I hope to date my next from some place up the country.

Adieu, and believe me yours ever,

S——.

The action that Saltoun referenced in his letter was a cavalry skirmish known as, 'The Battle of Morales de Toro', fought on the 2nd of the month. It took place north of the town of Toro which sits upon the Douro some distance east of Tordesillas. The 10th Hussars were in company with the 15th and 18th Hussars and their opponents were actually the French 16th and 21st Dragoons, under General of Division, Digeon. Though the forces were evenly matched in numbers (about 800 each,) the affair was a running battle in which the French were harassed severely suffering 200 casualties for just 18 British hussar troopers killed. One officer was also killed and two were wounded-one of them taken prisoner, presumably the Captain Lloyd, Saltoun mentioned.

CHAPTER EIGHTEEN

The Investment of San Sebastian, 1813

Wellington's main army, as previously indicated, took to the field whilst the Guards remained, for a period of time, in Oporto to recuperate from the devastating effects of the sickness which had significantly reduced their numbers.

Wellington initially decided to operate upon the French right, by marching through Tras os Montes in the north of Portugal. An army corps of five divisions, 40,000 strong, under Lieutenant-General Sir Thomas Graham, formed the left wing and crossed the Douro, reaching Braganza on the 22nd, May. Wellington advanced with 30,000 troops on Alba and Salamanca before turning north, uniting the two armies at Carcagales at the close of the month. The Spanish host under Freyre (Freire de Andrade y Armijo) likewise joined this principal force creating an Allied Army on the right bank of the Douro of 90,000 men and 100 guns. On the 4th of June, Wellington ordered its advance towards the frontiers of France.

Joseph Bonaparte was standing at Valladolid with 52,000 men and 100 guns, but could not long hold his positions for Wellington, by continually demonstrating towards his left, compelled him to withdraw. The rapid allied advance put the army at the Carrion on the 7th of June and five days later in sight of Burgos. The castle there was destroyed by the French before they promptly retired, anxious to place the defile of Parnorbo between themselves and the allies, but Sir Thomas Graham acting on the left, and marching by a route previously regarded as impracticable, crossed the Ebro at Frias on the 15th, and getting into the rear of the French right, cut them off from the coast. Wellington had gained a new base of operations on the sea, and the British fleet entered the harbour of Santander. The First Brigade of Guards were ordered to move up to the front at this point.

Sir Thomas Graham drove back Reille's corps, and on the evening of the 20th he halted at Marguia. Wellington gained a decisive victory over Joseph at the Battle of Vittoria on the 21st of June. For the French the defeat was cataclysmic. Professor Oman wrote:

> The defeated host had to retreat by the only route left to them, a rough mountain track to Salvatierra and Pampeluna, unsuited for the passage of an army encumbered with heavy impedimenta. The king had with him not only a vast train of artillery, but a great convoy of Spanish refugees—his partisans from Madrid—and countless carriages and waggons laden with treasure, pictures, state archives, and valuable property of all sorts, the accumulated spoil of six years of conquest. The whole of this heterogeneous mass of vehicles was thrown upon the narrow Pampeluna road, and hopelessly jammed within a few miles of its starting-point.
>
> The defeated army abandoned everything and fled over the hillsides. In actual casualties it had not lost heavily—some 6,000 killed and wounded, and 1,000 prisoners (of the 65,000 total); while the Allies had 5,000 men *hors de combat* (of the 80,000 total). But the French had saved nothing but their persons; the whole equipment of the army of Spain was captured by the victors, 143 guns, 500 caissons, nearly £1,000,000 sterling in the military chest, besides several thousand carriages laden with valuables. Seldom has an army shared such plunder as fell to the Allies that night. Thus, the vanquished French host reached Pampeluna in complete disorder.

Clausel and Foy retreated and, after throwing a garrison into San Sebastian, crossed the Bidassoa into France. Graham invested San Sebastian on the 9th of July, and on the 24th made an attempt to storm it, but the assault failed with heavy losses.

Soult arrived from Germany to take command of the French Army, and reorganised his forces advancing to attempt to turn the British right, relieving Pampeluna. Wellington converted the siege of San Sebastian into a blockade, met the French, and, after a series of combats which lasted from the 25th to the 30th of July, carried the position in front of Sorauren, forcing the enemy to retreat, and on the 2nd of August the French were driven across the frontier into France.

The siege of San Sebastian, following the initial reverse, was renewed, but hostile fire was not opened until the 26th of August. By this time the First Brigade of Guards arrived on the scene of action, and on the 18th of August marched into camp, joining the First Division.

★★★★★★

Leaving Lieutenant-Colonel Tinling at Oporto in charge of the sick, the First Guards, under the brigade-command of Major-General Lambert, began its march on the 29th of June, passing through Amarante, Villa Beal, Mirandella, Braganza and arriving at Palencia, on the 23rd of July. The men were in good health, marching well and not a single man was left behind.

From Palencia, instead of following the direct road to Burgos, the column took a northerly course, through Saldana to Reynosa and by Medina to Osona. The way was strewn with traces of the retreating French, and after marching over the battlefield of the 21st of June, the regiment passed through Vittoria. On the 10th of August it halted at Zobrano, and on the 11th passed by the Puerto de Francia, which contained a park of all the French artillery pieces, two hundred and ten guns, captured in the recent battle and during the subsequent retreat.

In his next letter to Catharine Thurlow, Saltoun's tone gave the impression he was somewhat 'war-weary' and, if this was the case, it is unsurprising for he had recently completed a long march to arrive at the site of a recently fought major action. The town of Vittoria was full of wounded—some of them Saltoun's personal friends and he also commented that there had been hard fighting in the mountains. It is noteworthy that Saltoun did not appreciate on this occasion (comparatively uncharacteristically given his usually astute and accurate appreciation of developing events) that the French were in irreversible withdrawal, since he appeared to have the expectation that the tide of the war would turn once again following a French counterattack designed to force the allies back into Spain.

Saltoun's report of the death of Cadogan was substantially accurate. The 71st Regiment of Foot was a Scottish Highland regiment that had been reformed as light infantry in 1810. Henry Cadogan fell, aged 34 years, as his regiment stormed the heights above the village of Puebla on the French left during the battle. He was a personal friend of Wellington and had fought a pistol duel on Wimbledon Common with Henry Paget, subsequently the Marquess of Anglesey (commander of cavalry at Waterloo), because Paget had engaged in an adulterous affair with his sister Charlotte, who was at the time married to Wellington's younger brother.

Durada,
13 August 1813.

My Dear Miss Thurlow,

We marched into this place yesterday, which completes our six weeks from Oporto. It is a small village, about two miles from Vittoria, on the Irun road. We halt here today, and tomorrow we proceed to the army, which we are to join on the 18th instant.

I went yesterday to Vittoria. It must have been a very fine town, but at present cuts rather a melancholy figure; not that it has been in any way destroyed, but it is a hospital for wounded, and has at present about 6,000 wounded men and officers in it, many of whom are just now beginning to walk, or rather crawl about; and so many poor maimed devils do not add to the beauty of a place. Several of them are old friends of mine, but all of them, I am happy to say, doing well.

I believe you knew Cadogan (Hon. Henry Cadogan, Lieut.-Colonel 71st Regiment, son of first Earl Cadogan) who was killed in this action. His death was one of the finest things possible. Being perfectly aware that he was mortally wounded, he asked the surgeon how long he could live, and was told about half an hour. He then desired the men who bore him to leave him for a short time. On their return he ordered them to take him to that part of the field where he could best see the British advance, and there died, just as the French line began to give way.

The second, fourth, and seventh divisions have had some very severe work in the Pyrenees, on the 27th, 28th, and 30th of last month, and the enemy were again completely defeated. You will, of course, have seen the details of these actions long before you receive this.

At present we are employed in fortifying the passes. St. Sebastian has not fallen yet, and I believe it to be a very strong place. If it does not fall before the 18th, we shall probably be employed against it. Pampeluna is blockaded, and they say that the garrison are very badly off for provisions, and that they have already begun to eat horse-flesh.

I wish it may be true, for if we can get possession of these two places, we may look to keeping the French out of Spain for this year at least, and next year the Spaniards *ought* to be able to do it of themselves; I say ought, not that I think they will, for they are even more indolent than ever.

By this time all the gay doings in town are pretty near over. I long much to get hold of my letters, as we have not seen a letter or paper from England since the 15th of June, and are quite in the dark as to what is going on in the north of Europe. But, however, in five days more we shall reach our division, and then I hope to have a letter of yours to answer.

Till then, *adieu*, my dear Miss Thurlow

Yours ever,

Saltoun.

On the 18th of August, the First Guards marched into camp at Oyarzun, two miles from Irun, and joined their comrades of the Second Brigade, in the left wing of the Allied Army under Sir Thomas Graham. Saltoun, of course, very shortly recommenced his correspondence with Catharine Thurlow. Having arrived at their destination, he appears be more business-like and was addressing himself to the soldiering requirements of moment. However, readers may be curious about his enquiry regarding 'the loo and Tabby set'. Loo or Lanterloo is a trick taking card game similar to Nap which was popular among society ladies at the turn of the 19th century in England. Dedicated rooms and tables for playing the game were created and the social circle of ladies who gathered therein were termed, not particularly kindly perhaps, 'tabbies', after a gathering of cats.

Camp before Oyarzun,
23rd August 1813.

My dear Miss Thurlow,

Yours of the 22nd June I only received yesterday, but I have written several times on our march, and mentioned that I did not expect to get any letters until we reached the army. A month is certainly a most unreasonable time for a letter to take from Oporto to England, but this, I trust, will make up for it; for I understand that the *pacquet* is ordered to Santander, which is but a short distance to send by land, and not above three days' sail to Falmouth.

We are quite quiet here at present, and likely so to remain, encamped on the Pyrenees, about three miles from Irun, at which place the bridge over the Bidassoa is destroyed. The French are on the opposite bank, and each party mutually fortifying his position. On our left, about five miles, is the seaport of Passages, so we are well supplied with fish, which is a great luxury, and ought to be also with English articles; but the sutlers have been so often taken in by the rapid movements of the army in this Peninsular War, that they are not inclined to risk any very great speculation.

St. Sebastian is about seven miles from this place, and is besieged by the Fifth Division, under General Oswald. A breach was made some time back, and they attempted to storm, but were repulsed with great loss. Since that time, we have been waiting for heavier guns and ammunition; the batteries are all ready. The guns and ammunition arrived yesterday, and on Thursday the 26th they are again to open against the place. It is of great consequence to take it, but it is very strong, and will cost a great many broken heads.

You wish to know what general we are particularly under; we are in the First Division, which is under General Howard (Lady Charlotte's husband), and the First, Third, and Fifth Divisions form the left corps of the army under General Graham. The Fifth, as I mentioned above, are against St. Sebastian, and we are covering the siege. The Third Division are on our right between this and headquarters.

We shall certainly not advance unless things go wrong in the north of Europe, and I do not think the French are strong enough to try another general action, as the ground in our front is very strong, especially that part which our division would probably have to defend should they attack the positions. By this time all the gaiety is over on your side of the water. I find her Ladyship has gone to the Lodge; I thought she meant at one time to go to Scotland this summer.

I wish you could persuade someone of our regiment to sell out. I am now first for purchase, and dread the tidings of peace more than anything; for then I should not get my promotion before it takes place, which would be a terrible bore, besides the length of time it would throw me back. However, I am not one of those who are apt to despair, and trust now to be home by Christmas as a Lieut. Colonel.

I am going today to see a friend of mine who was wounded the other day in the general action before Pampeluna. I do not know if you are acquainted with him. His name is Campbell, and he is Lady Malpas' eldest brother, a major in the 6th regiment.

Sir D. H. Blair and myself are old hunting friends. A few years back we kept house together for a season. The Vittoria *fête* seems to have been the great lion this year. It must have had a very grand effect; for of all places in London there cannot be a better place for a public sort of thing than Vauxhall; but to be good it ought to have been very full.

How goes on loo and the Tabby set? I dined yesterday with a man whom you must have often met there, Captain R—— of our regiment. He began to talk about Mrs H——, "a little woman with black eyes." I asked him where he had met her. He said he often met her at Mrs. P.'s, and that she was very fond of play, and led her husband a devil of a life. R—— and I happen never to have met at P.'s, and he little thought I could have given him tolerable information on that subject.

You see I take you at your word, and write as often and as long as I have anything to say; and it is accidental whether I have or not, for our life is either a very active or a very dull one, no medium.

I have written this on my knees, and I fear you will have some difficulty to decipher it, for my table, which cannot be very large in camp, is laid for breakfast, and four cups rather crowd it. We are going to have a rare wet day, but I must go and see Campbell for all that, as he is on his way to Bilboa, and I shall miss him if I do not. I hope to see you in less than six months. Till then, my dear, my dear Miss Thurlow, believe me, yours ever.

S——.

On the 28th of August the Guards advanced still nearer to Irun, acting as a covering force to the troops of the Fifth Division, who were carrying on the siege San Sebastian. The camp was well situated, about one mile from Irun, in an ancient wood upon the face of the mountain, from where the River Bidassoa, the French lines, St. Jean de Luz, and Bayonne in the far distance, were visible. The Second Brigade was encamped on the left of the First, whilst the Germans were in position to the left of the Second Brigade. The Bidassoa, from low water to half-tide, was fordable, but the ground in front of the Guards camp was very strongly defended, so there was little likelihood the enemy would attempt an attack from that side of the position.

Major-General Lambert resigned his command on being appointed to a brigade in the Sixth Division. Colonel Peregrine Maitland succeeded to the First Guards Brigade and Lieutenant-Colonel Hon. W. Stuart to the third battalion.

The left wing of the Allied Army, under Sir Thomas Graham, was now composed of the First Division under Major-General Howard; the Fifth Division under Major-General Sir James Leith; Lord Aylmer's brigade and a Spanish Army under Don Manuel Freyre. The Fifth Division, consisting of Major-Generals Hay's and Robinson's brigades, was engaged in carrying on the siege of San Sebastian while the First Division formed the covering force and guarded the line of the Bidassoa from the mountain to the left. Freyre's Spanish corps was posted to the right, on the heights of San Marcial. The order of battle of the First Division

176

was as follows: The First Guards on the right, Hinuber's Germans on their left, then Stopford's Second Brigade of Guards, and the German light infantry on the extreme left.

By the 30th of August the enemy's guns on the ramparts of San Sebastian were silenced, and as the walls had been breached in two places an assault was scheduled for the following morning. It had come to Wellington's notice that some officers of the Fifth Division doubted the practicability of storming the breach, and he felt that such demoralising views would inevitably have filtered down to the ranks creating a potential to turn prophecy into reality. He decided, therefore, to deploy volunteers drawn from some of his most reliable regiments for the task. Four hundred men would be taken from the First Division comprised of 200 men from the Division of Guards and 200 men of the King's German Legion and these would be combined with 350 men drawn from the Fourth and Light divisions to, as Wellington delicately put it, 'show the way to the breach if it should be practicable'.

The storming party of the Guards, consisting of 100 men from each of the First and Second Brigades, under the command of Lieutenant-Colonel R. H. Cooke of the First Guards, marched from their camp at six p.m., with the other detachments from the division, and encamped about two miles from the fortress. They moved off again about two in the morning of the 31st, and occupied the ruined convent of St. Bartolomeo, where they remained until half-past nine.

Sir James Leith, who commanded the assault, would not allow the volunteers to take the lead, placing them instead in support of Robinson's brigade. The troops advancing to the breach were exposed to a heavy fire and it soon became apparent that any concerns previously expressed with regard to the practicability of the breach were founded on nothing other than sound judgement, because it could only be accessed in single file which transformed its entrance into a narrow killing-ground. Nevertheless, the attacks drove forward in succession, and inevitably, acts of courage notwithstanding, all attempts to effect a lodgement foundered and

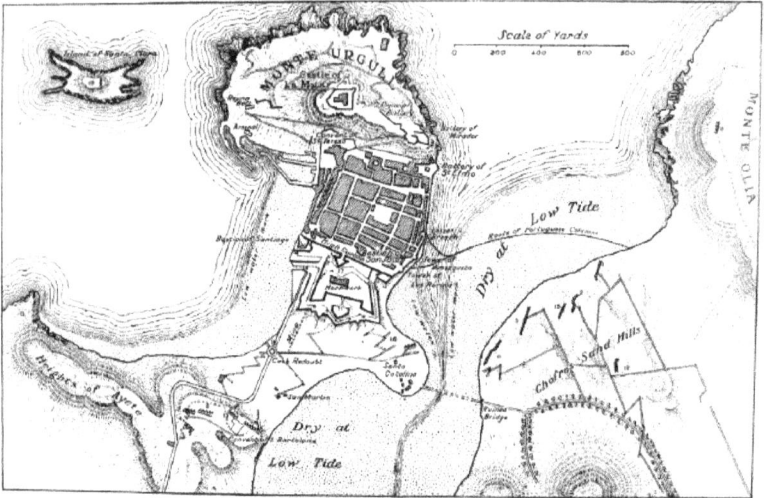

THE STORMING OF SAN SEBASTIAN

the stormers were mowed down in their hundreds.

The waiting volunteers impotently witnessed these events with mounting frustration and questioned 'why they had been brought there if they were not to lead the assault?' Finally, in the absence of any progress the volunteers were finally put to the task and they assaulted the breach ferociously, swarming up the ruins. After an initially promising advance, however, even this desperate attempt foundered and those that reached the crest were struck down leaving none but the dead or wounded remaining on the summit. Other attempts to break through followed, but fared no better than the first.

Graham, by this point realised that simply flinging human flesh at the fortified defenders was unlikely to result in success, so ordered the artillery to open fire over the heads of the assailants to clear the ramparts and as this barrage progressed, quite by chance, one shell upon impact ignited a quantity of gunpowder which the enemy had prepared to explode in *extremis* in the event that the ramparts were over-run. The resulting eruption literally and figuratively 'hoist the enemy by his own petard' and, taking advantage of the ensuing chaos, the British assault force finally burst through the French line to enter the town.

Saltoun did not take part in this assault with the Guards contingent. For that fact, both posterity and Miss Catharine Thurlow may possibly have reason to be thankful for these assaults were not termed, 'The Forlorn Hope', for nothing. Two days following the success at the breaches of San Sebastian, Saltoun once more faithfully put pen to paper in a letter to his 'dear Miss Thurlow'. Of the 207 Guardsmen of all ranks who marched to the assault, Saltoun with little emphasis, reported in his letter that just 50 of them returned to rejoin their comrades. The final section of Saltoun's letter on this occasion is particularly interesting and revealing since it describes an engagement undertaken by the Spanish Army under Freyre and Longa at San Marcial in which it acquitted itself very well despite suffering substantial losses; a phenomenon which is rarely positively reported in contemporary Peninsular War accounts written from British perspectives. Sir Howard Douglas, however, who had close associations with the Spanish soldiers during the war probably came close to the heart of the matter when he wrote, 'I must say they are well deserving to be better led. They possess all the qualities necessary to constitute a good soldier'.

Camp Irun,
2 September 1813.

My dear Miss Thurlow,

We came here two days back in order to support the advance, as the French were making demonstrations on this point with a view of preventing our attack on St. Sebastian; they had not, however, the desired effect, for we carried the place by storm at twelve in the day on the 31st instant. Our loss was very great; they rate it, as well as it can be now got at, to be about fifteen hundred men.

The place was stormed by detachments from the different divisions of the army, and by the fifth division under the command of Sir J. Leith, who is wounded. We sent a detachment of one lieut.-colonel, two captains, four subalterns, and two hundred men, fifty of whom have returned.

Of the officers, Burrard was mortally wounded, and died yesterday. He is son to Sir H. Burrard, the second he has lost in action in the regiment. Ensign Bridgeman slightly wounded, and Chaplin, who belongs to the Coldstream Guards, severely; he is shot in the breast, and his thigh broke so high that they cannot amputate; he is, however, doing as well as possible, but cannot be called by any means out of danger.

On the morning of the storm Soult made a general attack on our line, with an intention to relieve the place. The ground in our front is very strong, and defended by the Spaniards of the Gallician Army, under General Frere. The French attacked one hour before daylight, and carried a small height which they surprised; this enabled them to establish a bridge over the Bidassoa, and at eight in the morning they had passed over about ten thousand men, and made a regular attempt to carry the hill occupied by the Spaniards, without which they could not with safety pass any great force of artillery. The Spaniards defended it with great obstinacy, and about two, when the French had carried the hill, they made a very spirited charge, and with the bayonet drove them fairly to the bottom. Towards evening the French made another attempt, but a very feeble one, and on the Spaniards giving three cheers on being informed of the fall of Sebastian, they retired, and during the night took away the bridge, and have not since troubled us.

I have just come from the field, and from the number of dead lying there I should think the loss on both sides must be about five thousand men, of which number the Spaniards certainly lost the most. The French made an attack more on the right, and were met by the Seventh Division British, and repulsed with great loss. The castle of St. Sebastian still holds out, and will cost some more men; we are at present pounding away at it at a great rate.

I have now given you all the news, and must send this letter to Oyarzun to be in time for the mail if possible. I shall write should anything take place.

    Believe me, yours ever,

S——.

The French governor of San Sebastian, as Saltoun had indicated, retired to the citadel, and, on the 9th of September, after a spirited resistance of more than a week, surrendered. The casualties among the officers of the First Guards were one officer, Ensign Burrard, of the first battalion (son of Sir Harry Burrard), mortally wounded, and one officer, Ensign Orlando Bridgeman, wounded. Readers will recall that Burrard was an officer of the Guards and had been present in Portugal in the period leading to the infamous Convention of Cintra.

One of his sons had already been killed in action at Corunna in 1809 acting as an *aide-de-camp* to Moore and it is widely accepted that this second loss broke his heart for he was laid within his own grave in a little over a month. According to Lord Saltoun there were, in round numbers, 150 casualties amongst the 200 Guardsmen at San Sebastian. The total losses of the assault were in the region of 1,500 men though the cost of defeating the French in the town must have been twice that number.

Soult made one more attempt to relieve the fortress on the morning of the assault, by threatening the allied left: but it was easily repulsed. During this attempt the First Division was drawn up in support, in the rear of Irun, but was not engaged. The enemy withdrew over their frontier on the same day. By this point, France was beset on all sides by both land and sea. Napoleon's hubris had led him to monumental ambitions which not only over reached his considerable resources, but led him to squander them. The disastrous retreat from Russia had cost him an enormous army, rewarded him with nothing and laid the foundations for his fall.

Prussia had joined the Russian alliance ready to take the field, and Austria was also covertly preparing to recommence hostilities. Irrespective of the emperor's failures as a strategist on the grand scale he remained a formidable campaign and battlefield commander by comparison with practically every adversary who might come against him. Napoleon, rapidly collected another army of 200,000 men and 350 guns, with which, in May 1813, he fought and brilliantly won the battles of Lutzen and Bautzen in Germany. However, the abiding fact was that the allies would never cease to oppose him until they were done with him and the encouraging news from Spain was a further indication that the First Empire of the French had never been more vulnerable. Austria once again actively rejoined the allied cause, as it was always bound to do, had taken to the field, but was resoundingly beaten at Dresden on the 27th of August, with heavy losses.

Nevertheless, undaunted the allies immediately rallied and, gathering a host 250,000 strong, came to the fray once again to oppose Napoleon at Leipzig and after three days' gruelling combat between the 16th-19th of October, gained a decisive victory, which obliged the French Army to retire across the Rhine. Determined now to follow through with their advantage, the allies doggedly pursued it crossing the north-eastern borders into France in several places. Napoleon had not fought his last battle, nor won his last battlefield victory, but his time was running short and he was now at bay, his enemies were closing in upon him and his nation was tired of war and the perpetual sacrifice of its sons on the altar of his megalomania.

CHAPTER NINETEEN

The Pyrenees—The Bidassoa, 1813

By the end of September, the siege at San Sebastian was over and the British Army had marched away from it leaving the Spanish to garrison and repair their town and its fortifications. Saltoun, in his regular correspondence with Catharine Thurlow, described the scene in the aftermath of the battle perfectly from the perspective of the British regimental officers. Either because he was astute or because the 'telegraph' of the army ensured practically everyone knew what was happening at the time and what would happen next, he demonstrated his typically accurate assessment of current affairs.

Saltoun referred to a forthcoming trip to visit Sir Rowland Hill at Roncesvalles with his friend and brother officer, Edward Stables, who would be killed in action at the Battle of Waterloo.

One aspect of the following letter, however, is particularly interesting since it bears directly on the behaviour of British troops in extreme circumstances. This was a subject upon which Saltoun had decided opinions and, indeed, he had previously written about it in the strongest terms; bridling at Wellington's accusations of a negligent failure in control of the men by their own officers. He reported that after the British troops had entered San Sebastian they had, true to form and past experience, run riot and thoroughly plundered the place, 'in the most barbarous fashion and set fire to it'.

Whilst his condemnation of this sacking of another Spanish town was unequivocal, there was nothing in his comments, on this occasion, to suggest that he did not expect what would happen when the town eventually fell. Furthermore, he raised no suggestions for a systematic preventative measure that might be instituted, as he had by contrast, on the privations of the troops on the retreat from Burgos. In short, he mentioned the fact, but did not make much of it.

That troops were given a period of latitude to despoil a town they had taken by storm after severe losses was a very long established aspect of warfare and, despite their personal opinions on the matter, commanders at this time apparently still accepted it was necessary to tacitly allow (if not condone) and a price to be paid irrespective of whether the place belonged to an ally. The engaged troops likewise expected this 'reward' as their due during this period and retained the inclination to indulge themselves in ghastly full measure. The author has no intention to put a modern moral cast upon these matters, other than to note they significantly speak to the nature of British society and its relationship to the army at the beginning of the 19th century.

Camp Irun, Spain,
26th September 1813.

My dear Miss Thurlow,

I received yesterday, and am most happy to find that our letters on the march have arrived at last; for I began almost to despair about them. You have, I believe, two more still to receive at least. We halted twice between Toro and this place, and I usually wrote on those days, and did not leave you out.

Since my last, which was after the fall of Sebastian, we have been quite quiet in this part of our line—indeed I may say all along the line—and have been employed fortifying the position. You do not seem to like the marching much, and I think working would be still less agreeable to you; not that we officers work, but we are obliged to see that the others do. Since it has begun, this is the first day that it has missed me, and I have generally had the morning party from half-past five till twelve; very pleasant amusement standing on a hill for six hours seeing two hundred men dig, especially in this beautiful climate, where we never have two fine days running. I never in my life was in such a place for rain, and further on the right it is worse.

I wish the *Beau*, as his Lordship the Field-Marshal is called, would cross the Bidassoa and move down into France, as then, at all events, we should not be regularly sluiced night after night in our tents, which is the case here; for no canvas, nor anything else that ever was invented, will stand the rain in these hills, and we have famous fun with the gentlemen amateurs from England with their water-proof coats and *ne plus ultra* pelisses, which they find of very little use here, and they must be content, as we are, to get wet with philosophy, and dry as soon as they can.

Tomorrow I set out on a trip to the right. I mean, if I can, to get as far as Roncesvalles, where Sir R. Hill is stationed, with whom I am acquainted. I mean to see the ground of the late actions, the finest ever fought by the British yet, and on the most extended scale of military operations.

I have a good many friends to call on in the way, which will make it a very pleasant trip. Colonel Stables goes with me, and our leave is for eight days, should the army make no movement, which it probably will not till our redoubts are finished, and they cannot well be complete before ten days more, and then I hope we shall make a start.

Sir James Leith, who was wounded at the storm of Sebastian, is doing very well, and will soon be fit to join his division, which belongs to our column of the army, and, to use the military phrase, is closed up, that is, has encamped in our rear, ready to support us if necessary. They marched from Sebastian the day before yesterday, and that place is now given over to the Spaniards, who have placed a garrison in it, and are to repair the breach. It was a very fine town, but I am sorry to say our troops plundered it in the most barbarous manner, set fire to it (or, as some say, did not put out the fires which caught accidentally). Be that as it may, they have not left a single house standing in it; the Turks could only have done that.

I know Mr. Joliffe, though I am not acquainted with him. Who does not know him, at least his hat, which is tolerably con spicuous! He keeps a pack of hounds, and I have always heard is an excellent good fellow. I must finish this, for the post leaves Oyarzun at three, and now it is past two, and it is more than a league from hence to Oyarzun.

Adieu; and believe me, my dear Miss Thurlow, ever yours,

S——.

The fall of San Sebastian occurred five or six weeks before the pivotal engagement at Leipzig and during the interim, as Saltoun's letter amply illustrates, Wellington remained inactive. His circumstances were, however, about to change fundamentally, for any advance from his present position could not be defined as the expulsion of an invading army from the territory of an ally, but as an invasion of another country by forces under his command. This was not necessarily a straightforward matter under the circumstances, since political consideration as to whether France should actually be invaded was an issue which occupied the sovereigns of the coalition of allies in the northeast and no policy had yet been decided upon it by them.

The military question was should Wellington advance into France before the allies made their own advance given this would create a beneficial diversion which would work in favour of his own operations? The British Government eventually solved his dilemma for him by instructing his own advance to provide the diversion to assist the continental allies, who were, in fact, preparing for the great blow against the French emperor which would become the Battle of Leipzig. Accordingly, Wellington early in October, forced the passage of the River Bidassoa and marched his army, for the first time, onto the soil of Southern France.

The mountains of the Western Pyrenees rose opposite the Anglo-Spanish position, separating the valleys of the Bidassoa and the Nivelle rivers. Wellington's plan was to seize, with his right and centre, the highest point of these mountains—La Rhune (now Larrun), and its dependent ridges, while on his extreme left, he would obtain possession of Fuenterabia. The French position to the north of the Bidassoa was naturally formidable and Soult had further strengthened what nature had provided with additional defensive works.

The French dispositions anticipated that their enemy would attack their centre and left, but the ever-observant Wellington grasped the potential to neutralise Soult's dispositions by passing the army over the mouth of the Bidassoa at low tide. At the crossing point the tide rose sixteen feet, and the sands were half a mile wide. The First Division and the Fifth Division, together with Portuguese troops, which formed the left wing of the Allied Army, were nominated to carry out this part of the attack. This audacious manoeuvre would both surprise and outflank Soult rendering his defence redundant. Bold though this initiative was, it was not without risk, because it would not be long after the troops had crossed that the tide, rising once again, would isolate those on the enemy held shore with no hope of retirement or succour until the next ebb tide, by which time Wellington's intentions would be fatally revealed.

Two brigades of Guards and Brigadier-General Wilson's Portuguese brigade would cross over the Bidassoa, by a ford close by a ruined bridge and also by two fords a short distance down the river. The lowest ford was called the Vado de las Nasas de Abaxo, and was near the point where the *chaussée* from Irun arrived at the banks of the river itself. Some of these battalions were to pass at a ford a short distance above the ruined bridge, and all were to advance upon the fords to coordinate with the time that the Fifth Division from Fuenterabia would move forward. Assembly would begin before dawn, near Irun, and all movements were to be kept concealed until the moment of the simultaneous attack and ford crossing.

A rocket from the steeple of Fuenterabia would signal the advance for the brigades of Guards to coincide with the movement of the Fifth Division. Elements of the cavalry from the 12th Light Dragoons, with the brigade of artillery attached to the First Division, and a brigade of reserve artillery, were to cross the river with these columns. Other guns were to cover the passage from the most available heights of San Marcial, on the reverse slope of which, Alymer's brigade formed the reserve to the First Division.

The first objective of the Guards after crossing was to establish themselves upon the opposite hill known as Montaigne de Louis XIV. and on other high ground, keeping up a communication on their left, if possible, with the Fifth Division. The troops were all to be in position at seven o'clock in the morning, since low water arrived at a quarter past the hour. At three o'clock in the morning of the 7th of October the First Division was under arms and marched off. It passed through Irun, arriving at the rendezvous point on time, unobserved by the enemy, the manoeuvre covered by a violent thunderstorm which fortuitously burst over the French position. The advance began and the fords were approached without an angry shot having been fired as a certain indication that the French had been taken totally by surprise.

Meanwhile, under cover of heavy artillery fire from the heights of San Marcial, the right column of the First Division, comprised of Wilson's Portuguese, supported by the two battalions of First Guards, crossed the river in front of the lower heights of San Marcial, taking the higher right hand fords and advanced towards the enemy. Once upon the opposite bank it drove the French from the village of Andaya and advanced rapidly towards Croix de Bouquet. The left column, Second Brigade of Guards, preceded by the KGL light infantry, crossed the river at the ford, near the broken bridge, and formed on the right of the Fifth Division, covering the building of a pontoon bridge so artillery could also move up.

The eighteen-year-old, Rees Howell Gronow had joined the First Guards as an ensign in February, 1813 and after a few months of mounting guard at St. James' in company with his young, fellow officer friends, Dashwood, Batty, Browne, Lascelles, Hume and Master he joined a detachment of five hundred men bound for Spain. The crossing of the Bidassoa was his first experience of a military campaign and he later made a note of it in his reminiscences.

> Our regiment advanced through difficult country and after a harassing march reached the top of a hill as the grey light of morning began to dawn. We marched in profound silence, but with a pleasurable feeling of excitement amongst all ranks at the thought of meeting the enemy, and perhaps with not an equally agreeable idea that we might be in the next world be-

PASSAGE OF THE BIDASSOA, OCTOBER 7TH 1813

fore the day was over. As we ascended the rugged side of the hill, I saw for the first time, Wellington. He was accompanied by the Spanish general, Alava, Lord Fitzroy Somerset, and Major, John Freemantle *(Wellington's ADC and private secretary, then 23 years old).*

We commenced the passage of the Bidassoa about five in the morning, and in a short time infantry, cavalry and artillery found themselves on French ground. The stream at the point we forded was nearly four feet deep, and had Soult been aware of what we were about, we should have found the passage of the river a very arduous undertaking.

Three miles above we discovered the French Army and ere long found ourselves under fire. The first man I ever saw killed was a Spanish soldier, who was cut in two by a cannon-ball. The French Army, not long after we began to return their fire, was in full retreat and after a little sharp, but desultory fighting, we took possession of their camp.

Success was, as Gronow reported, virtually immediate and the French forces before Maitland's First Brigade of Guards promptly fled leaving three guns behind them, whilst the left column of the First Division drove the enemy from the Café Républicain and the Montaigne de Louis XIV. The attack swept on to Croix de Bouquet, which was the key of the position and after a severe struggle, the heights there were won. The enemy, outflanked by the left column of the Fifth Division also gave way. The First Brigade of Guards, advanced and encamped for the night on the heights they had won, to the right of the high road leading to Urrugne.

During the advance of the First Guards light infantry, under Saltoun, they passed some French wounded soldiers lying by the road side. To his horror, Saltoun witnessed one of his men walk towards to one of them in particular, and after pausing for a moment, drive his bayonet through him. Saltoun immediately rushed up to the offending guardsman and demanded to know the reason for such barbarous behaviour towards a helpless incapacitated Frenchman.

'It's no Frenchman, sir,' was the indignant reply; 'it's that 'Ev-

THE GUARDS CROSSING THE BIDASSOA BY ROBERT BATTY

ans' who deserted the night before the Battle of Corunna.' The wounded man was sent to the field hospital for treatment, but died the following day of his wounds. The accusation had been correct. This 'Evans' had, indeed, deserted his regiment nearly five years previously in January, 1809, had taken service with the French at the commencement of the war, and now, towards its close, in 1813, met his death from the hands of his former comrades, by whom he would not have been recognised, had he not, on seeing the uniform of his old regiment, imprudently called out to them for a drink of water.

The fighting had been more severe on the right of the British line, though the French there were also taken by surprise. The Light Division and Giron's Spaniards assaulted the ridge called Bayonette held by Taupin's division, carrying it, in spite of the height of the mountain and strength of the works. Freyre's Spaniards had, in the meantime, assaulted the Mandela heights, and, by advancing on St. Jean de Luz, by Joliment, cut off Taupin's line of retreat. The French had succeeded in repelling the attacks made upon the great Rhune Mountain, but abandoned its defence on the following day.

The army suffered less than a thousand casualties in the affair and the First Guards suffered no loss at all during these operations; the Coldstreams had 2 rank and file killed, and 8 wounded; the Third Guards, 9 rank and file wounded, and 2 missing. The French casualties were over 1,500, but they significantly also lost 14 cannons.

CHAPTER TWENTY

The Nivelle, 1813

Since the British Army was now in complete possession of the formidable position the enemy had occupied the day before, the French begrudgingly retired and took up a new position for the defence of the line of the River Nivelle.

The health of Sir Thomas Graham had been failing for some time so he resigned the command of the left wing the day after the passage of the Bidassoa. In fact, Graham genuinely believed he was (and wished to be) done with soldiering permanently, but before long fate had another military expedition in store for him. He was succeeded by Lieutenant-General Sir John Hope, who had arrived from Ireland on the previous day. This was the Hon. John Hope, ultimately Earl of Hopetoun who had taken command at Corunna after the death of Moore. Other 'John Hope's' had previously served in Spain as divisional commanders, notably at the Battle of Salamanca in 1812, where there had been two of them.

In view of the close proximity of the armies, there was much outpost duty for the light infantry companies of the Guards, and the advanced sentries of the opposing armies often stood at night within thirty yards of each other. Naturally, Saltoun was engaged on picquet duties with his men and at the end of the first week in October he took the opportunity during one such night to write a letter, once again, to Catharine Thurlow. In it he explained his own part in the passing of the Bidassoa and once again he made a comment on the good performance of Spanish troops. In centuries past Spanish regiments enjoyed the highest reputation during the wars in Europe and much concerning their poor performance during the earlier stages of the war in the peninsula bore on the quality of political and military leadership in Spain.

He began his letter with a reference to the 'Song of Roland' which concerns the defeat of the Charlemagne's army under the heroic Roland by the Basque Army in *A.D* 778. The conflict at Roncesvalles in 1813 occurred when the French under Reille and Clausel advanced with 40,000 men against Lowry Cole's, Fourth Division of 11,000 men which was defending the pass. Cole withdrew in the direction of Pamploma.

Camp Urogne, France,
9th October 1813.

My dear Miss Thurlow,

As we are now proudly fixed in France, and being on picquet within a very few yards of the enemy, and therefore not willing to sleep, I cannot employ myself better than letting you know how we have been going on since I wrote last.

I mentioned that I was going to take a trip to the right of the line with old Stables, which we put in force the next day, and were very much pleased with it. The scenery is of the grandest kind, most particularly the valley of the Alduides and that of Roncesvalles, famous in former days for the fight which we have both heard remarkably well said or sung by poor C. Anguish in these times; not less famous for one of the sharpest affairs that have lately taken place in the Pyrenees; but except at Astley's or Sadlers Wells I much fear it has a bad chance of being again remembered in poetry, unless it should graciously please Walter Scott to give us another part of Don Roderick's Vision, for which he has certainly now sufficient materials.

The Pass of Roncesvalles lies over a very high mountain, the top of which is in our possession; at the bottom of it, on the French side, is the town of St. Jean Pied de Port. This pass forms the right of our line. In the valley, on the Spanish side, stands the convent in which they show you Orlando's club and armour. It is beautifully situated amongst large woods of old beech trees, and open patches of old parkish ground, the arrangement of which would have made the fortune of any capability gentle-man in England—the whole closed, in the grandest manner, by the mountains. From this pass, coming to our left, the next pass is the Alduides, which is very beautiful, but not so grand as Roncesvalles. From that, passing by the Puerto de Viscayret, you reach the Pass of Maya, and so by the Pass of Echallar and that of Vera, to Irun, to which place we returned on the 5th.

On the night of the 6th we got our orders at twelve to at-tack the next morning, and at three in the morning of the 7th marched to our points, so as to reach them before daylight, that the enemy might not observe our movements, and at a quarter before eight, it being then low-water, forded the Bidassoa in five columns, and advanced against their position, the enemy making but little resistance, being partly surprised; for our plan of attack was so well combined that his position was turned and attacked, hill after hill, nearly at the same moment.

He ought, however, to have defended his position—which is a very strong one—with greater obstinacy. Our loss was small—between 300 and 400 men, I should guess. At twelve we had gained our present position, just above the town of Urogne, which is now the French advance, and before dark were quietly encamped upon it. During the time that this operation was go-ing on, the Light Division debouched by the Pass of Vera and attacked the Hill of Urogne. which is a high mountain on the right of our present line, and carried it in good form.

The poor natives are terribly alarmed, and have all fled; not that they fear us (the English), as they have given us to un-derstand, but they know well the way their troops treated the Spaniards, and they dread the retaliation which they know they deserve from the troops of the Peninsula, whom a year back they looked upon as slaves, called them brigands, and treated worse than dogs, and if they made them prisoners, for it was seldom that they gave quarter to a Spaniard, and the poor dev-ils, from wounds or sickness, could not reach their destination, regularly shot them; and the Spanish soldiers have not forgot it. And although as yet I do not think they would stand hard squeezing, they behave well, mixed as they now are with us, and face their enemy in a better style than I ever thought they could be brought to do.

Everything looks as if we were to make a forward movement,

and I trust my next will be dated from some place further in the heart of France. we can see a long way into the country from our present position, and it appears to be a beautiful and rich country. I shall go on scribbling for ever, but I am sure by this time you must be tired of army speculations, which are but dry ones at any time.

I have just heard that a mail has landed, and I hope to have a letter tomorrow when I am relieved.

You most likely are just now going to bed, so goodnight, and believe me yours ever,

S——.

In a letter home written by Lord Saltoun at the end of October, and also sent from camp above Urogne he describes a very interesting incident that personally concerned him as he served with his men of the light infantry company in close contact with the enemy on outpost duties.

We have a great deal of duty; our light infantry do the advanced duty and no other. I am on every fourth day; and the posts are so close, our advanced sentries at night standing within thirty yards of each other, that both parties are tolerably alert; indeed the Germans, who take that duty with us, and who have been all their lives on that species of service, say they never saw posts so close, without a ravine or brook, or something of the kind, between them, which is not the case here.

Upon one occasion, when I was in command of the outposts of our brigade, I was going my rounds with a small escort very early in the morning. Our sentries and those of the enemy were at no great distance from one another, and I noticed that one of the French sentries, who was posted on a rising ground affording some view of the country beyond, appeared to be asleep. I determined to surprise him if possible, and obtain a look at what might be the scene of our own operations in a few days. Taking one of the escort with me, and leaving the others to watch, he and I crept, as if deer-stalking, towards the sentry, and managed to reach him without awakening him. He reclined with his back to a tree, against which he had leant his musket, and of this I quickly made myself master; then, while my companion kept guard over the still sleeping sentry, I examined the country beyond with my glass, and got a good deal of information as to its nature, the disposition of the enemy's troops, etc. etc.

I intended at first to go back without wakening the Frenchman, and to take his musket with me; but reflecting on the severe punishment, perhaps even death, that would await him if discovered by his own officers in that state, and without his arms, and noticing that he was a young soldier, I could not find it in my heart to do so, and we therefore awakened him. His surprise and horror may be more easily imagined than described, and if we had not held him down and stopped his mouth, he would have bolted shouting an alarm.

When he became a little calmer, I said to him, 'My friend, it is far better for you that I have caught you asleep than that one of your own officers should have done so; now, no one will know of it unless you tell, be more careful in future, and keep better watch; I return you your musket, and shall trust to your honour not to fire at us as we retire.'

However, not to depend too much on his honour, I took out the flint, and shook the powder out of the pan before giving it back to him. He seemed very grateful, and thanked me most warmly, and then we rejoined our party.

A few nights after this I was again in command of the outposts, and wishing to visit another post at some distance, I set off on horseback alone. The night was pitch dark, and I lost my way, and got close to the cordon of French sentries, when my horse, crashing through a slight hedge, half scrambled, half fell into a hollow road; and at the same instant came a challenge from the top of the opposite bank, '*Qui v'là?*' and I heard the ring of a firelock brought to the ready.

I sang out, '*Officier de la poste Anglaise,*' and explained that I had lost my way in the dark. The French sentry asked if I was hurt by the fall; and on my replying, 'No,' that I was all right, he most civilly directed me how to get within our lines again; and as we parted said, 'I am happy to be of this service to you; we have all heard of the kindness of one of your officers the other day to a young sentry of ours that he caught asleep.'

I told him that I was the officer in question. 'Ah!' he said, 'that makes me doubly happy, that is the way brave enemies should always treat one another;' and so we parted excellent friends, and I found my way by the directions he had given me.

To this time Pampeluna remained in the hands of the French and Wellington was keenly aware of the potential threat this enemy concentration posed were he to advance before the city was taken. In fact, ultimately no blood was spilled in reducing Pampeluna, because, after a most effective blockade which lasted four months, the French, all but starved into submission, surrendered on the 31st of October, securing the Anglo-Spanish army's position to carry the war into the enemy's territory.

Saltoun's letter to Catharine Thurlow originally dated the 31st of October was written over a period of days and reflects the changing position that occurred during that time because at the letter's outset Saltoun comments, 'as soon as this confounded place, Pampeluna, falls', whereas the latter section, dated November 6th makes it clear that the news of Pampeluna's fall had by that time reached the army. Readers may note Saltoun's romantic closing paragraph of his letter in contrast to what he would write to her a few months afterwards.

Camp Urogne, France,
31st October 1813.

My dear Miss Thurlow,

Yours of the 4th of this month I received a few days ago, enclosing a map most beautifully drawn on silver paper, and I have compared it with the large French map of the Pyrenees, and, considering the scale, it is tolerably correct as far as Maya, but it takes no notice of the valley of the Alduides, nor that of San Carlos, which are leading features in the frontier line between the valley of Bastan and that of Roncesvalles, and are divided from each other by the large mountain of Arola. The situation of the towns on the Spanish side is tolerably well laid down, as well as in most maps; and with respect to the French side I will tell you a little more when we have advanced further up the country, which we shall do as soon as this confounded place, Pampeluna, falls.

Our army is in exactly the same position as when I wrote you last, the left on the sea-coast above Urogne, extending to the right through Zagaramurdi and Urdax to Roncesvalles, which is our right. The right of the French rests on Fort Seres, the centre at Mondarin, and the left at Arosa and St. Jean Pied de

Port. On the Nive River, on their right, they have a second line from Mondarin through St. Pé to St. Jean de Luz, on the small river Nivelles, which is not fordable from St. Pé to the sea except at low tide.

They are doing everything in their power to fortify this position, and all our arrangements are complete for an attack, which will take place as soon as Pampeluna falls, which cannot hold out above a few days longer; indeed we have been in treaty for the place, but the terms that the garrison wanted were, to be sent to France not to serve against Great Britain or her allies for the space of a year and a day. These were, of course, rejected; and after a little more starvation they will surrender at discretion.

November 6th—I was obliged to leave off to go on duty, and as tomorrow is post-day, and I have very little news, I shall tack it on here.

Pampeluna surrendered a few days back; the garrison were 4200 strong, and when they gave in, they had had nothing to eat for three days. Poor devils! how very thin and genteel they must have looked when they came out after four months' low diet. I should not admire the starving much; a siege is bad enough, but a starving bout is ten times worse.

As yet we have made no movement in consequence of the weather, which has been so bad for some days back as to put a stop to all military operations, by rendering the roads impassable for artillery, and the rain has swelled all the small rivulets so much that the troops cannot ford them; besides, what is rain in our part of the line is snow at Maya and Roncesvalles, but yesterday and the day before were fine, and the weather seems again to be settled.

All the arrangements for a start are complete, and we expect our orders to attack hourly. I do not expect we shall have much to do in the first instance, as the position opposite us will be turned by our right, and the enemy must either abandon it, or if he resists stoutly (which, by the by, I do not think they are in a good humour for at present), he must be made prisoner in it, and it is not their game to lose men in that way, for they have not too many to spare now.

I am on the outposts, and we have just had a parley with *Johnny Crapeaux,* (the French officers) who has been sending in money to some of their officers who were wounded and taken when we crossed the frontier. They have no later news from Napoleon than ourselves. No news, they say, is always bad news for them. The officer I spoke to was at Moscow last year; he is very tired of it, and wishes to go into winter quarters. I told him we had no such word in the British service, and that we meant to be in Bayonne shortly, and perhaps Bourdeaux, on which he vociferated, "*Sacre F——*," and strutted off in grand style.

I am not much inclined to be civil to these rascals, for I hate them most heartily, and they swagger and *cut a big swell* on these occasions, which at present is rather our right than theirs. Some of them, however, are very gentleman-like men, and then are pleasant fellows enough.

Our posts at this part of the line are so close, that the French and our picquets at night are not more than twenty yards from each other, and no obstacle between, which makes desertion very easy, and many of our Germans who have been enlisted from the prisoners of war go off, and a good many of the French come over to us; one came in last night. He says that they are very badly off for bread, but have plenty of meat, and, generally speaking, are very dissatisfied.

You wish to know why I put a little S in the corner of the direction? it is a trick that one gets from writing reports, as it is customary to put your name on the outside, which acts as a pass for the soldier who carries it, in case any post should hesitate to pass him; and when I am afraid that my letter may not be properly directed, I always write my name on the outside, as from its being known at the post-office, they return me the letter without opening it, which is rather an advantage than otherwise.

Before you receive this, you will be thinking of returning to town; I should have no objection to be there with you, in spite of what I told the French officer; and believe me, my dear Miss Thurlow, ever yours,

S——

The French position now before Wellington extended from St. Jean de Luz on the sea coast, on their right, eastwards for about twelve miles, to the hills in front of Souraide and Espelette. The whole enemy defensive line was strengthened by earthworks. The left of the French first line rested on the River Nivelle, extending to the right of the Choupara and Mondarin mountains, while Clausel's corps occupied the heights of Ascain and Arnots, between which were the camp of Sare and several strong redoubts.

Since the passage of the Bidassoa, Wellington noted that Soult had secured his right flank by a triple line of defensive works in front of St. Jean de Luz on the Nivelle. These would have made a frontal assault so costly that, once again, a more imaginative solution was required to affect the British Army's advance. Given this problem was exactly the same kind of situation that had inspired Wellington's plan for passing the Bidassoa, one may have supposed Soult would have foreseen what alternative approach might be instigated by his opposite number. That solution proved to a combination of a feigned attack made by his left wing, now under Hope, while Wellington proposed to force the enemy's left, and threaten the rear of his right, which would compel him to withdraw from St. Jean de Luz, once again abandoning redundant works.

Hope was to operate in three columns. The left column, composed of Halkett's German light infantry, was to act between the heights of Urrugne and the coast, fronting northwards towards Socoa Fort; the centre column, or Fifth Division, and some other troops were to occupy the most advantageous points upon the left bank of the rivulet, which runs between the heights of Urrugne and those of Siboure, and when halted were to face towards Siboure and St. Jean de Luz, while the right column, composed of the two brigades of Guards, were to threaten the front of the French encampment on the right bank of the rivulet of Urrugne, and on the British right of the high road leading from that village to St. Jean de Luz, keeping up at the same time the communication on their right with Freyre's Spaniards, who were to attack Ascain.

The First Division remained under the command of Howard, while the First Brigade of Guards was commanded by Maitland. Heavy rain initially delayed the attack but, in the early morning hours of the 10th of November the weather eventually cleared. During the previous night the army, with approaching 100 guns,

BATTLE OF THE NIVELLE, NOV. 10TH 1813

British

Spanish and Portuguese

Closed works with artillery

Entrenchments

Inundations

moved quietly and undetected into their positions.

At about three a.m., the First and Fifth Divisions moved down the heights and advanced to the line of outposts, arriving about an hour before dawn. The French picquets of the advanced posts of Reille's and Villatte's divisions, were strongly entrenched, and a large redoubt defended the rising ground in front of Urrugne. At the signal of three guns fired from the Alchabia mountain, the massed allied artillery opened up on the French position, and the army began the attack. On the left, Halkett's German light infantry moved round the hill, whilst the picquets of the First Division, under Lieutenant-Colonel West of the First Guards, made a rapid attack in front, driving the enemy from his advanced position down the hill to the entrenchments,

The brigades to the left of the First Division moved directly upon Urrugne, while Maitland's Brigade of Guards and Hinuber's King's Germans advanced against the heights behind Urrugne, which extend towards Ascain. The First Guards and German light infantry kept up a continued fire, but, as per Wellington's intentions, they received no orders to storm the works before them. Hope, however, had now gained the heights commanding Siboure, so that he was in a position to take advantage of any forward movement the right centre of the enemy might make. He kept up this false attack until nightfall, compelling Reille's and Villatte's Divisions to engage him and so preventing them from sending assistance to Clausel commanding the centre of the French Army.

While the First and Fifth Divisions held their ground on the left, the balance of the army advanced, driving the enemy from their positions and seizing the bridges of Ascain and Arnots over the Nivelle. The French fought stubbornly, but at last retreated, abandoning their entrenched camp of St. Jean de Luz. During the action, Soult arrived with a large body of troops at Serres, and threatened the allied centre, but the position of Hope's wing prevented his aiding Clausel. At the close of the action Hope followed the retreating French across the river.

The brigades of Guards were not significantly engaged in

the main involved and in consequence their losses were trifling, but Captain Charles Allix, First Guards, acting brigade-major of the First Brigade, was severely wounded, and Captain William Miller took his place. Miller would fall, mortally wounded at Quatre Bras.

CHAPTER TWENTY-ONE

The Nive & St. Pierre, 1813

The French Army again withdrew, taking position on the heights of Bidart on the road to Bayonne, where it prepared to defend the passage of the Adour, and on the 11th November the British Army, in turn, moved forward to take it to task. The First Division, after passing over the now abandoned fortified position in front of St. Jean de Luz, sighted the town at midday, descended into the valley, forded the river and advanced to within eight miles of Bayonne. The First Guards' Brigade took post on the right, a mile or so from the high road. The enemy's right rested at Anglet; their centre on the ridge of Beyres, and their left on the entrenched camp of Bayonne, situated near the confluence of the rivers Nive and the Adour.

Bayonne was covered to the south by an entrenched camp created by the genius of fortification, Vauban. Soult's right, in the form of three divisions, under Reille, was concentrated touching the Lower Adour, and supported by a flotilla on the river. A swamp covered his front, and several fortified posts were positioned forward near Anglet, two miles from Bayonne. Clausel's three divisions extended from the entrenched camp to the Nive, covered partly by the swamp, a fortified house, and an inundation near Urdanis; D'Erlon's four divisions extended up the right bank of the Nive; D'Armanac was in front of Ustaritz and Foy, at Cambo.

Wellington, needed to extend his line from his position between the Nivelles and the Nive and took the decision to cross the River Nive, so as to establish himself on the left bank of the Adour. The weather remained too poor to ensure the operation had its best opportunity for success, so the First Brigade of Guards was returned to St. Jean de Luz, and was quartered in the suburb of Siboure.

An officer of the Guards, writing from St. Jean de Luz on the 28th of November, after giving an account of the state of affairs, referred to a rumour he had heard that Napoleon was coming to Bayonne to personally take command of the French armies.

> I am sure that there is not a man in the army, from Lord Wellington himself to the lowest soldier that would not think it the happiest day of his life to be fairly placed in front of the French with Bonaparte at their head. If ever there was a day when British soldiers would be more than themselves, that day would certainly be the one.

Time, marching its inexorable course, was taking that officer towards the day when at last he and all the players of this drama would be together in the fields beyond Waterloo. Whether that day would, indeed, transpire to qualify as, 'the happiest day of his life', remained to be seen. For the present, Wellington intended to pass the Nive with his right wing, and place it on the Adour. Meanwhile, Hope would demonstrate with the left wing of 24,000 men, against the entrenched camp at Bayonne, occupied by Reille and Villatte so as to mask the actual objective of the manoeuvre. Having assessed the position and strength of the enemy in front of Bayonne, Hope was then to reconnoitre the mouth of the Lower Adour, with a view to throwing a bridge across it.

The brigades of Guards paraded in the early hours of the 9th, before an arduous march through wet and overcast weather along the coast road to take up their position. The brigades halted at Barouillet, in front of Bidart. The Fifth Division then crossed the valley between Biarritz and Bidart, with its left resting upon the coast.

At eight o'clock the First Battalion, First Guards advanced, covered by the light infantry and by artillery fire. Shortly after

First Foot Guards in winter dress

the engagement began the enemy stubbornly retired and by one o'clock, the light infantry had driven the enemy through the village of Anglet and down the slopes of the entrenched camp. The First Division had taken the heights on the right of the road near Anglet.

While the attention of the French was focussed on Hope's army, Hill and Beresford were able to pass the Nive near Ustaritz and Cambo. There the enemy fell back without a fight, and so Wellington succeeded in gaining a position for his operations against the French left. At about six o'clock in the evening, he directed Hope's successful troops to return to St. Jean de Luz. The Fifth Division, which formed the rearguard, halted at Bidart, leaving a Portuguese brigade in advance at Anglet. That night the First Brigade of Guards, under Maitland, reached its former quarters at Siboure, the southern suburb of St. Jean de Luz.

Wellington's left was now in a potentially perilous position since it was separated from the rest of his army by the River Nive, and Soult was not slow in appreciating that fact nor in imaginatively seizing the opportunity it presented. He marched from Bayonne on the morning of the 10th of December, at the head of 60,000 men, against Hope's wing. Reille, driving the Portuguese from Anglet, advanced towards Barouillet, while Clausel on his left attacked Arcange, occupied by Kempts' Brigade of the Light Division, which held its ground all day. The sound of heavy firing from the front announced the seriousness of the conflict and in due course, an *aide-de-camp* arrived, warning the Guards and the troops in the rear, that the attack was a dangerous one. The Guards advanced quickly to the scene of action and took their place in the battle line.

However, the difficult terrain had prevented the enemy deploying effectively, the attack had been repulsed, and its renewal was discouraged by the arrival of three divisions near Ustaritz, on the left of the enemy's attack. The First Brigade, however, remained that night in Bidart.

The French again attacked the outposts of the left wing on the 11th, and after passing the flanks, penetrated the first line,

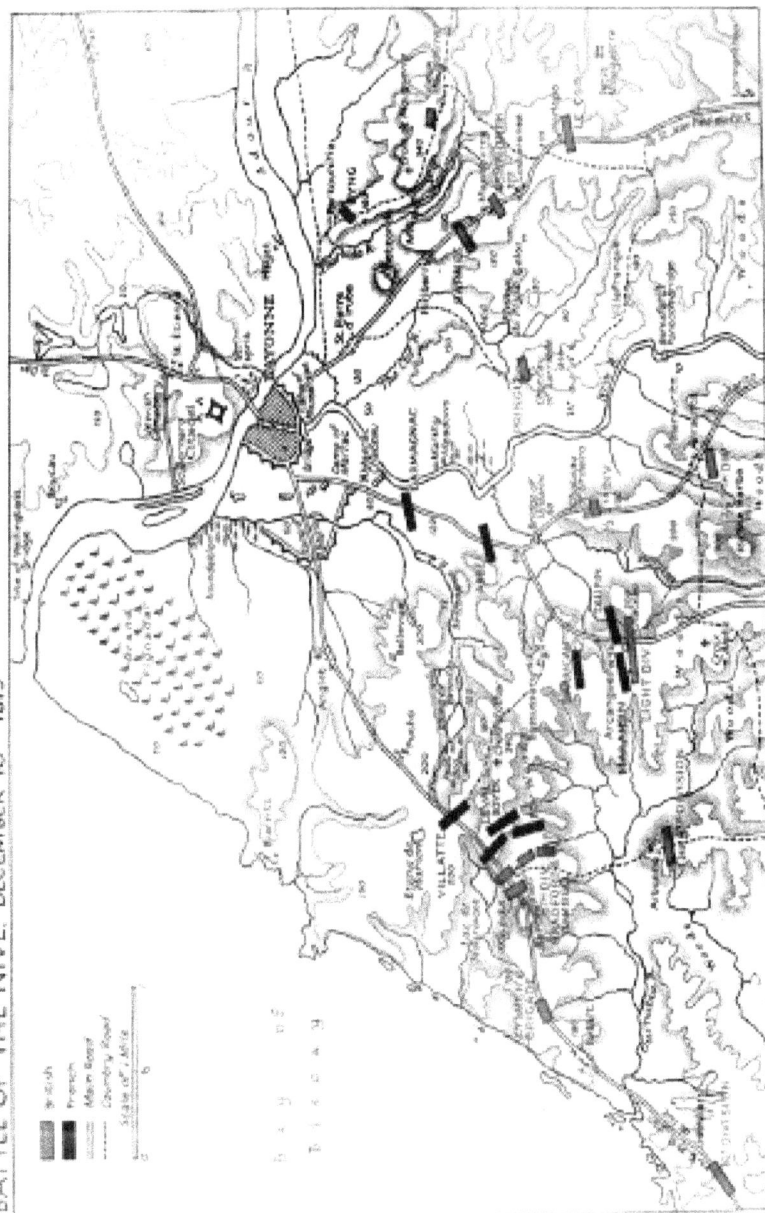

BATTLE OF THE NIVE. DECEMBER 10TH 1813

but when Aylmer's brigade arrived, Soult withdrew his troops behind the Etang de Chartreuse, opposite Barouillet. The Guards relieved the Fifth Division in the front line that night, which then formed on the ground which had been recently vacated by the Guards.

The two brigades of Guards took a position in front of Barouillet. The First Brigade, under Maitland, stood near a farmhouse on the brow of a hill, separated by a narrow ravine from the heights which were still held by the French. The picquets of the Third Battalion, First Guards were posted in a thick coppice wood on the slopes of the hill, while those of the first battalion, on the extreme right, commanded by Captain West, were in a large orchard to the right of the farmhouse. The First Battalion, First Guards, under Colonel Askew, was formed on the high ground to the rear, while the third battalion, under Colonel Stuart, was to the left, in rear of the farm, with some artillery. A picquet of the First Guards, under Lord Saltoun, occupied a hut to the left, to watch the road which led from the enemy's position, and to keep up the communication with the Second Brigade, in front of the mayor's house. Rees Gronow, in his recollections, gave a first-hand impression of the fighting:

> The Guards held the mayor's house and the grounds and orchard attached. Large bodies of the enemy's infantry approached, and after desultory fighting succeeded in penetrating our position, when many hand to hand combats ensued. Towards the afternoon we drove the enemy from the ground they disputed with us and then retreated towards Bayonne. Every day there was constant fighting along the whole of the line.

The night of the 11th was overcast and wet, and at day break the French appeared in force with more troops coming up from the rear. About ten o'clock, a strong line of French *tirailleurs* advanced from the west along the brow of the ravine in front of Maitland's, First Brigade of Guards. The artillery opened fire and brisk skirmishing continued throughout the day in front of both brigades causing a loss of about 200 officers and men. Lieutenant-Colonel Coote Martin, commanding the picquets of the First Battalion, First Guards, was shot down in the orchard and almost immediately afterwards Captain Charles Thompson, of the same battalion, was mortally wounded, while leading his men. Captain Streatfield was slightly wounded about the same time, whilst Ensign Lautour also took a severe wound.

Marshal Soult discovered he could make no impression on the allied left, under Sir John Hope. The British position on the left bank of the Nive was secure, with the likelihood that it would be further strengthened. Accordingly, Soult temporarily retired behind his own entrenchments. His next plan was to leave a deceptive cordon of outposts in front of Hope's troops, but to covertly pass 35,000 men quickly through Bayonne during the night, with the intention of attacking Hill's corps the following morning on the right of the Nive. Marshal Beresford, with three divisions, was dispatched early in the morning of the 13th, to Hill's assistance. That general had only 14,000 men under him, but he held his ground at St. Pierre, and repelled every attack, though the struggle at one point became critical, until Wellington arrived with the reinforcements.

The French attacks then became gradually feebler, and at two o'clock Wellington ordered a general advance. The French retreated, fighting hard, and during the night Foy's division retired across the Adour, and were sent to reinforce Reille, opposed to the British left. While the fight was raging at St. Pierre on the 13th, the enemy reinforced their advanced posts in front of the First and Fifth Divisions, and firing was kept up with little intermission till the afternoon. The First Brigade of Guards, the Coldstreams, and Lord Aylmer's Brigade took the brunt of the conflict and Captain Carey le Marchant, of the 1st Guards, *aide-de-camp* to Lieutenant-General Sir William Stewart, was severely wounded.

Saltoun's next letter to Catharine Thurlow begins with a description of the recent fighting which is, the reader will note, very accurate in its appreciation of the action, though in typical style he coolly and dispassionately relates the facts rather than emphasising that the battles around the Nive and at St. Pierre in particular were hard fought. The British regiments, despite the outcome, had been severely tested. Indeed, some writers claim that this fighting represented some of the most brutal of the entire Peninsular War.

Soult had demonstrated a particularly innovative tactical ability on this occasion and Wellington had been, if temporarily, wrong footed. In the end, Wellington's soldiers won the victory for him in the manner which he freely acknowledged they dependably would, even when he had made a mistake. The French marshal was not so fortunate and these operations cost him between six and seven thousand men. To make matters worse Napoleon then ordered Soult to release 10,000 troops to serve on the eastern frontier, leaving him with less than 50,000 men which amounted to a little more than half of those that Wellington had at his disposal.

Soult's weakening position was further exacerbated by the desertion of whole regiments of German troops who served the imperial cause begrudgingly and were quick to abandon it now that it seemed the end of French dominance was at hand. Saltoun reported this detail at the end of his letter to Catharine. The Nassau troops were particularly highly regarded by both the French and the British in Spain. Wellington is on record of expressing his high opinion of them and, in due course, Saltoun would know their worth more intimately, for they would be fighting on the allied side very close to his own post at Hougoumont before a year and a half had elapsed.

> Camp before Bidart,
> 13 December 1813.
>
> You see, my dear Miss Thurlow, we are again under canvas, and have had some sharp work for these four days past; we have had two officers killed, and two wounded. I do not know if you are acquainted with any of them;—Captain Martin and Captain Thompson are killed, and Captain Streatfield and Ensign Latour wounded, the latter severely. We have lost one hundred and fifty men.
>
> Old Soult has been manoeuvring and trying to deceive Lord Wellington, by showing a large force at different points of our

line. On the 9th we advanced and attacked in front of this place, and drove the enemy into his strong ground in front of Bayonne; in the meantime, Sir R. Hill crossed the Nive at Ustaritz, and rested his right flank on the Adour, so as to intercept Soult's supplies, which he received from Pau and Oleron by that river. This obliged Soult to make some decided movement, and on the 10th he attacked us, but was repulsed by the Fifth Division. On the 11th he again attacked us, and got a hill in our front that covered his movements. That night we took the outpost duty, and on the 12th he appeared in force, and manoeuvred under cover of a very sharp affair of *tirailleurs*, but finding us well prepared at all points, he during the night recrossed the Nive, and on the 13th made three desperate attacks on Sir R. Hill, and was defeated and driven into Bayonne with great loss. I do not know what our loss has been on the right, but I understand very small in comparison.

Fortunately, the weather has been fine, and still continues so to be, but very cold in the tents at night; however, anything is better for soldiering than wet, and I dare say it will be some time before we again go into winter quarters, if we do so at all.

I have not had any letters from home for some time, but I understand that my mother has not as yet got her house settled, and moreover is very likely to lose it. I see your cousin the Lord is married by the papers.

The news from the north is very good, and has spread through France; for the day before yesterday three German regiments in the French service—one of Nassau, the others of Baden and Frankfort—came over to us with their officers, arms, and every other necessary; they are marched to Passages to embark for England. This shows that the morale, as Napoleon calls it, is not the same in the French ranks as formerly, and I very much suspect that the material is almost as low.

I have no more news to tell you, so *adieu*, and believe me, my dear Miss Thurlow, yours ever,

S——.

Rees Howell Gronow of the First Guards was present when some of the Germans, who were apparently expected, came over to the British lines. In his reminiscences he wrote:

Shortly before we left St Jean de Luz, we took our turn of outposts in the neighbourhood of Bidart, a large village about ten miles from Bayonne. Early one frosty morning in December, an order came that if we saw the enemy advancing, we were not to fire or give the alarm. About five we perceived about two battalions wearing grenadier caps coming on. They turned out to belong to a Nassau regiment which had occupied the advanced post of the enemy and hearing that Napoleon had met with great reverses in Germany signified us their intention to desert. They were fine looking men and appeared, I thought, rather ashamed of the step they had taken.

The First Brigade of Guards returned to St. Jean de Luz after these actions, and as the final days of 1813 were allowed to pass by without any aggressive demonstrations from the French, the new year began with Wellington establishing a firm foothold for his army upon enemy soil. Portugal and Spain had seen the last of the emperor's machinations, though the legacy of the turmoil he had wrought upon the Iberian Peninsula would mean that years of strife lay ahead.

CHAPTER TWENTY-TWO

The Forcing of the Adour

On the first day of 1814, Saltoun dutifully penned a letter to his, 'dear Miss Thurlow' and he opened his correspondence, as usual, quite charmingly whilst giving the impression that both he and his lady—though apart—were engaged in recreational expeditions in 'the country'. However, when Saltoun more soberly turned his attention to military matters and the consequences of an imminent closing of hostilities, he once again revealed himself to be prescient, for he expressed the opinion that if Napoleon were to be given access to 300,000 released French prisoners of war it would be but a matter of time before he once again employed them as an army in war.

Indeed, Saltoun believed that Napoleon would not, in this conflict, be comprehensively beaten and so a British Army would be certain to fight him again in the future. The accuracy of his forecast in the light of future events requires no emphasis, though given the convoluted course which brought the emperor to his final battlefields in Belgium, it is quite remarkable that it was made a year and a half before the fact. Of course, Saltoun thoughtfully closed his letter, as he began it, with news of a social occasion. The days of peace would indeed soon come, but would be as short lived as winter sun.

St. Jean de Luz,
1 January 1814.

My dear Miss Thurlow,
Since I wrote last, which was after our brush on the 12th, I have

received yours of the 30th November, by which I see you have returned from your expedition to Hampshire, which I hope you found much to your satisfaction, and at all events had better weather than we had here about that time.

Since I wrote you nothing has taken place with us in the fighting line; but for all that we have not been perfectly quiet, for it pleased Soult to cross the Adour in force on the 3rd instant, above the right of our army, and accordingly on the 4th we were all put in motion, and both armies continued manoeuvring until the 8th, when Soult retired across the river and resumed his old position; and today we have followed his example and taken up our old cantonments. At one time on the 7th he had very nearly put his foot into it, and Lord Wellington would have attacked him on the 8th, but he found it out in time and was off during the night. We have fortunately not had a great deal of rain, but it is very cold lying out at this time of the year.

I begin to think the war seems drawing to a close, but I hope we may take the field once more, and put the thing past a doubt by forcing Napoleon to make peace on French ground; for when he receives back the prisoners of war that we and the allies have taken from him, we give him an army of at least 300,000 men, and set him up at once as a formidable enemy, long before the nations wrested from him can reach their place in the scale, as he has taken care to drain them pretty handsomely during the time they were under his dominion; and even Austria will be a long time before she recovers from the great losses she has sustained in this and the last war.

Little England, however, can hold up her head and say, we have beat you at last and will have at you again as soon as you please, for in peace where France gains ten, we gain at least a hundred for the first years of it. I have given you a tolerable dose of my ideas of affairs in general, and shall leave off, but will not finish this till tomorrow, when the post goes, in hopes of having something more to send.

Another mail has arrived from England, but brings no particular news. . . . We are to have a grand ball here tonight—about two hundred men in fine coats, and certainly not more than ten ladies, including chaperones; not very gay, but it serves to pass the night. *Adieu*, and believe me, my dear Miss Thurlow, ever yours,   S——.

Soult strengthened his position, beyond the rivers Bidouse and Gave d'Oleron. On the 3rd of January, 1814, he attacked the British position on the Joyeuse, and shortly thereafter appeared in front of the left wing of the army. In response to this development, the Guards were despatched from St. Jean de Luz to the outposts of Barouillet, where they relieved the Fifth Division, which then took ground to the right to await the onslaught. No French attack materialised however, so the Guards marched back to St. Jean de Luz, leaving the outposts to Lord Aylmer's brigade. On the 14th of January Aylmer was relieved by the First Guards, who were in turn relieved by the Second Brigade.

The construction of a line of entrenchments for the defence of the ground behind Barouillet along the front of the left wing occupied the following days for the British troops and the drudgery of the chore was impeded, and made the more miserable, by perpetually wet weather that dragged on through the remainder of the month. Furthermore, the left wing of the army was detailed to take part in the investment of Bayonne, which not only removed it from operations under Wellington's immediate command, but prevented its involvement in several more influential actions at Orthez, Garris, Aire, and Tarbes.

Unexceptional as January, 1814 was for the First Guards, there was one ray of sunshine for Saltoun for he realised his ambition for promotion. Accordingly, the light companies of the Brigade of Guards were now placed under the command of Lieutenant-Colonel, Lord Saltoun, who had been promoted to command a company at the end of the year 1813. This promotion would, under normal circumstances, have returned him to England to serve with the home battalion, but this outcome did not suit him. He applied instead to continue on active service as the commander of the light companies, though notably the details of his deliberations before the fact of this decision, for perhaps obvious reasons, had not thus far featured in his correspondence to Catharine Thurlow. He would only reveal his decision when the deed was done. Towards the end of January, he wrote a fairly usual letter combining light hearted news with that of the progress of the army. His post script is worthy of note since this engagement would lead to the disastrous assault on Bergen-op-Zoom

St. Jean de Luz,
30 January 1814.

Yours, my dear Miss Thurlow, of the 4th I received a few days ago.

It had been a most enormous time on its passage, as indeed have all the packets lately; for it is the latest packet we have from England, and now we have two due, and a third will be so in a few days. I cannot conceive the reason of it, as the wind with us has been northerly for some time past, and Admiral Pickmore has arrived in a ship-of-war, and he left Plymouth on the 20th. Some people say that the road to Falmouth is snowed up, and therefore the mail cannot get down; be that as it may, it is very provoking, as I expect to get my promotion every day, and of course, you may suppose, look anxiously for the packet.

I find old Hughes is a very general favourite; he is quite well, and when sober as good a servant as ever, but he has learnt to cure sore backs of horses and mules, which in this army is a very common complaint, and he, James Hughes, having gained the name of a good doctor, is consulted on every occasion, by which means he picks up so many shillings and so many friends, that he gets drunk now past all former example.

You are quite correct as to the country being swampy, but it is not by any means unwholesome, for the army never were known to be so healthy as at the present time; and excepting the regiments just come out from England, we have no sick in the army. It is in the summer, when these swamps are nearly dry, that this sort of country is unhealthy.

I will refer to the little map, but I much fear we are out of the district it particularly notices. Our left is at Bidart, extending to the right by Arcangues and Arauntz, crossing the Nive River in front of Ville Franche, which is in the map, so on to the Adour River by St. Pierre, also in the map, to Petite Moguere on the Adour. We then take the course of the Adour River to Urt, where Sir Stapleton Cotton is stationed with some cavalry and the Third Division of infantry, to watch the movements of General Arispe, who is at St. Jean Pied de Port with two divisions, and we shall most probably remain in this position for some time, as the immense quantity of rain that has fallen within this week has rendered the roads almost impassable.

I had a letter from my mother the other day; she likes Brighton very much, but I think her house is in very bad hands as far as expedition goes. We must soon have peace; all the French papers talk of it as a certain thing.

Adieu, my dear Miss Thurlow, and believe me ever yours,

Saltoun.

P.S.—We have just heard that our army in Holland has been engaged;—*Viâ* France.

Readers will have noted that in his letter, Saltoun referred to James Hughes, who was his servant and clearly someone that Catharine knew. Hughes was apparently quite a character and something of a reprobate. He served with his master in the Peninsular War and during the Campaign of 1815. In this narrative he will, therefore, appear again.

Saltoun's next letter to Catharine Thurlow, written a week later, is an interesting one. One may imagine its author had deliberated how best to break the news it contained to the two most important women in his life which was that, far from coming home to them as his recent promotion allowed, he was, by his own choice, to remain in the field. Without doubt he knew this was the last place either of them would prefer him to be, particularly as the war appeared to be drawing to a close for there is a particular tragedy in being among the last to die.

Evidently Saltoun came to the conclusion that there was virtually no way the blow could be softened and so he decided to directly inform them of the harsh truth of the matter. He knew well that tears would probably be shed over his letter by Catharine Thurlow and perhaps it is for that reason that for the first time in his correspondence to her he elected to associate his name and hers with the word, 'love'.

This small detail, without doubt, would not have escaped the recipient of this letter since it would have been, from her perspective, its single redeeming feature.

St. Jean de Luz,
6th February 1814.

My dear Miss Thurlow,

You, of course, before this time, know of my promotion, and perhaps are among the number that expect me home; but if so, you will be disappointed, at least for the present, for I have accepted the command of the Light Companies, in which I have always served, and mean to remain with this army till the thing is decided, which must be the case, one way or the other, in a very few months, and then I shall return without the certainty of being sent out again immediately.

This is not any sudden idea of mine; for I had settled in my own mind, when I left England, if I got my promotion not to go home. I never mentioned it to my mother or you, because, although I knew it to be perfectly right in me to do so, I should have had some difficulty in persuading you of that.

Now, however, that it is past altering. I think I could persuade you that it is correct for me not only to serve with a good grace when ordered, but, at the present time especially, to show that I am willing and ready to serve without being compelled to do so; and I have accordingly made an offer of my services to the Commanding Officer of the Brigade, who has been pleased to accept of the same, not but what I would give a great deal for one fortnight in London, if the fog was ever so thick.

Indeed, I look forward to nothing with so much pleasure, and it must soon happen, for things are now come to such a pitch, that we must have a close in a very few months. I have written this in the most horrible hurry possible, for the post is ordered out today an hour sooner on account of the bad roads, so must conclude with hopes of very soon seeing you, notwithstanding my volunteering, and with loves and affections, etc., believe me, my dear Miss Thurlow, ever yours,

S——.

Wellington was aware that Soult imagined his defensive positions beyond the Adour were practically unassailable. Nonetheless, the French marshal knew he must expect an attack somewhere from the British before much time had elapsed. Whilst any such advance would be problematic, it was acknowledged that one of the least tenable places to attempt a crossing of the

Adour, French opposition notwithstanding, would be at the river's mouth below Bayonne. This consideration, persuaded Wellington (as it had Wolfe at Quebec in 1759 concerning the cliffs to the Plain of Abraham) to select that option for his *coup de main*, since it would also certainly be the least well defended. Accordingly, forty ordinary French trading vessels, or *Chasses-Marées*, were gathered for the operation at Socoa, near St. Jean de Luz. Whilst the rumour was spread about that their purpose was to serve the commissariat, they were actually to be employed for the construction of a bridge of boats to span the river.

The first part of this operation was to convey confusing signals to the French marshal by means of feints and demonstrations. During the second week of February, while Hope, with his left wing, showed a bold front towards Bayonne, Hill attacked. On the 16th of February he drove the French advanced posts back to St. Palais, on the Upper Bidouse. Marshal Soult then retreated behind the Gave d'Oleron, with his left resting on Navarreins, leaving a garrison under Thouvenot in Bayonne.

Meanwhile on the 15th of February, the two brigades of Guards, under Maitland and Stopford, advanced to the plateau near Biarritz, and took up a position facing the town with the rest of Hope's troops; the First Brigade, on the right of the road to Bayonne, also occupied the *château* of Pucho. The Fifth Division, on their right, extended from Bussussary to the Nive, while Hinuber's Germans and Stopford's Second Guards Brigade were on the left.

The light companies of the Guards, and the light battalions of the German Legion, were on the advanced posts; the sentries of the First Brigade being posted a short distance from Anglet, which was occupied by the enemy, while Aylmer's brigade with Campbell's Portuguese were in support at Bidart.

It was from this position, with the light companies, which were Saltoun's new command, that he wrote a letter to Catharine Thurlow. The letter reveals that the location of the coming assault was not only a secret, but on this occasion a well-kept one. Predictably, everyone had their own ideas as to where the actual crossing would be made and speculation ran so high that bets were being taken on the subject. Perhaps at this point, having read several of Saltoun's predictions, we should not be surprised that his own conjectures (and perhaps familiarity with the methods of his general) led him to forecast the correct conclusion. This letter, though begun on the 17th of February, was not immediately despatched and contains another section dated the 25th of February which will appear in its proper chronological place.

Heights above Anglet,
February 17, 1814.

My dear Miss Thurlow,

We marched out from St. Jean de Luz on the 15th and occupied these heights, our left resting on the sea in front of Biarritz, and communicating with the Fifth Division on our right in front of Arcangues, who extend to their right as far as the Nive River, and the Sixth Division occupy the ground between the Nive and the Adour. The Light, Second, Third, and Fourth Divisions, with a strong force of cavalry, have moved upon Hasparen and the River Aran, and the French have retired from their position on the Aran, and occupy one on the Bidouse, which they will also retire from.

All this is preparatory to our crossing the Adour, which we shall do in a few days, and probably without being opposed, but at what point nobody at present knows, but most probably at more than one place.

In the meantime everybody has his own particular favourite points, which he will back against any other; or taking the odds against the field—and they vary as they do in the Derby or any other event—my points are the junction of the Gave and the Adour, and at the mouth of the Adour, if possible; but the difficulty at the mouth will be very great, owing to the great width and the force of the tide, which is here very rapid; but should the weather continue as fine as it has been for these six days past, we may pass it anywhere, as the necessity of the high road will be done away with, for the guns will be able to move by the cross-roads, which during the rainy weather were perfectly impassable.

Sketch Map of the
Country round Bayonne.
showing the Passage of the Adour.
& the events of December & February 1813-14.

Allies ■■ French ⬜

BATTLE OF ORTHEZ
FEB. 18th 1814

PASSAGE OF THE
ADOUR FEB. 23rd
24th. 18 Jan. 2 ...

St. Etienne

Pierre
DEC. 10th - 1813

NIVELLE NOV. 10th 1813

BATTLE OF THE
NIVELLE NOV. 10th 1813

River Adour

Gave de Pau

Gave d'Oleron

Heights of Mugron

(This letter was concluded on February 25th—see following)

A week later Wellington was ready to put his plan to force the crossing of the Adour into action. At midnight, on the dark night of 22nd of February, Sir John Hope ordered the advance of 28,000 men, including the two brigades of Guards, twenty guns, a rocket troop, and eighteen pontoons. As the force approached Anglet, the First Division, (silently for the enemy sentries were barely a musket shot distant), turned to the left towards the coast. The track the column trod was narrow and muddy, with deep ditches on either side, which perhaps inevitably eventually upset an 18-pounder gun causing frustration and delay. Stopford's and Hinuber's brigades moved towards the mouth of the river with the pontoons, and at daybreak Saltoun's light infantry of the First Guards advanced along the plateau, driving the enemy from Anglet into their camp.

Maitland's brigade followed, advancing through the Bois de Bayonne, dragging the 18-pounders with them, and debouched near to the eastern beacon. Here they formed under cover of the sand hills, close by the marshes, on the western front of the enemy's camp, opposite Boucant. The guns were put in position on the extreme left, near the Adour, fronting the right flank of the enemy's camp. The First Guards, with their guns, were now in a position to prevent the French from hindering the building of the bridge and to suppress enemy fire as troops began to cross over it when it was completed. The enemy's gunboats and a frigate stationed on the river at once opened fire on Maitland's men, but intense return fire from the British gun battery and rocket troop drove the vessels away.

Plans on a grand scale that require precision timing are apt to go awry and so the hope that the *Chasses-Marées* would arrive at the required location at the same time as the column with the pontoons was possibly always overly ambitious. In the event bad weather delayed the arrival of the vessels which necessitated a display of initiative on Hope's part. Aware that his window of opportunity was short, he determined to press ahead with the attack and effect the crossing with the means he already had at hand. Whilst the First Brigade worked hard to engage the enemy's attention, a pontoon raft together with some boats, succeeded in conveying a small force under Stopford, comprising six companies of the Third Guards, two of the Coldstreams, and two of the 60th Rifles, over to the right bank where they were fortunately put ashore unopposed.

The French column, under General Thouvenot, who appreciated that the pivotal moment had arrived, advanced to the attack in the fading light of the day, with drums beating the *pas de charge*. Stopford's men, held their fire until the enemy column was almost upon them and then delivered a barrage of rolling fire to its front, while the rocket troop (giving a notable demonstration of the effectivity of Congreve's invention when well managed) and guns on the sand hills on the southern bank opened a devastating fire upon its left flank. Gronow reported the event in his reminiscences:

> Sir John Hope ordered our artillery and rockets, then for the first time employed, to support our small band (on the opposite shore). Three or four regiments of French infantry were approaching rapidly when a well-directed fire of rockets fell amongst them. The consternation of the Frenchmen was such, when these hissing, serpent-like projectiles descended, that a panic ensued and they retreated.

The enemy was, indeed, comprehensively routed, and on the following morning the 24th, the remainder of the Second Brigade of Guards, the Germans, and Portuguese successfully crossed over the river under the protection of both the beachhead force and the artillery protecting their flank. An imaginative plan implemented by bold and adaptable commanders on the scene had brought the day to a successful conclusion at very little cost.

The delayed flotilla of *Chasses-Marées* eventually appeared in the Adour at midday on the 24th and the construction of the bridge began immediately. The boats were anchored forty feet apart, about three miles below Bayonne, and the enemy once again missed its opportunity and did nothing to prevent or impede the work. The First Brigade of Guards were the last of the First Division to cross over, though since the bridge remained under construction it was compelled to utilise the raft and boats first employed. This proved to be a drawn-out affair since the raft was soon put out of action by the rapid tide and only twelve men could cross at a time in each of the boats. So, it was dark before the last men of the brigade were ferried over, and by that time it became a struggle to prevent the boats from drifting out to sea.

(Saltoun completed his letter to Catharine Thurlow with yet another accurate forecast of developing events)

February 25th, before Bayonne—We crossed the river the day before yesterday in boats, and are now in position round Bayonne, and have cut them off from all communication with their rear. We passed, as I conjectured, at the mouth, and I think our bridge of boats will be completed tomorrow, when the remainder of our cavalry and artillery will pass. It is not as yet known whether we are to besiege the citadel or not, but I begin to think we shall. Lord Wellington has not as yet crossed. I have not time to write a long epistle, as I am in command of the advance posts and wanted every minute. *Adieu*, and believe me ever yours,

Saltoun.

CHAPTER TWENTY-THREE

The Investment of Bayonne,1814

As Saltoun had predicted, Hope lost no time in investing the citadel which was positioned on a bend on the right bank of the river. The Bayonne citadel is a formidable fortification designed by the redoubtable Vauban, known as 'The Father of the Star Fort', and built during the 1680's for Louis XIV. At seven o'clock on the morning of the 25th of February, the First Division and Bradford's Portuguese advanced in battalion columns of companies. The First Guards on the right, with their right resting on the Adour, halted for a short time at Boucant, while the centre and left brigades moved round, forming to their right, till the extreme left rested on the Adour above the town.

While this was going on to the north of the river, the Fifth Division, which still remained on the south bank, crossed the Nive, and took up a position between the Nive and the Adour. The French garrison was now effectively isolated, though, for the British, surrounding a fortification and causing one to fall remained two entirely different matters.

An attack was also made on the enemy's entrenched camp, to discourage them from interfering with the bridge of boats. Work on the bridge was completed by the morning of the 26th and it remained operational till the end of the war for traffic between the Spanish frontier and Bordeaux. The obligations of his duties had prevented Saltoun from writing a missive of his usual length to Catharine Thurlow and his next short note was clearly hurriedly penned to ensure that it was included in the post which was about to depart. Readers of the history of the Peninsular War as it was fought in this period will be familiar with the word 'Gave'. A gave is a river of any size within the Pyrenees region probably derived from the pre-Celtic *'gaba'* meaning a banked river. Since they have their sources in the mountains, they are invariably not navigable, fast flowing and the banks can be problematically very high.

My Dear Miss Thurlow,
26th.—All quiet here this morning, and the letters will go off in about ten minutes. We yesterday heard from Lord Wellington. He has passed the Gave D'Oleron without opposition, and is to pass the Gave de Pau today. Nothing as yet determined about this column, and I do not suppose it will be for a day or two. You will probably see Reeve, who has gone home, at least if he remains any time in town, as he is a great dandy. Her Ladyship *(his mother, Lady Saltoun)* is still at Brighton, and I rather think that the house will go against her whenever the Chancellor takes upon himself to determine it. She must find it a great bore, for in the present state of affairs she cannot look out for another house, for fear this suit should go in her favour.
By-the-by, I see your cousin has been publishing again in verse, and not much better than the first production. I have not been in bed these four nights, nor shall I be as long as I am in command of this post, as we are rather too close for regularly going to bed. It is now after daylight, and about my time for taking a regular good snooze; so I have tolerable good practice in late hours, and shall be a match for anyone when I return. . . .
   Ever yours,

S——.

Once the bridge was secure, Hope began to contract his lines round the citadel. The enemy had strongly entrenched himself under the protection of guns from the fort in the village of St. Etienne, situated on a ridge, along which ran the roads from Bordeaux and Peyhorrada.

The troops moved forward in three columns, converging on the citadel. The right column, consisting of the two battalions First Guards, advanced in *echelon* of battalions from the left; the third battalion leading, halted for a time on the slope of some high ground, followed by the first battalion. The enemy opened fire, and as soon as the first battalion had crossed the marshy ground in its front, Maitland moved his whole brigade forward together, covered by light infantry, and drove the enemy back into their entrenchments.

The brigade was now within 900 yards of the citadel, the right resting on the Adour, at the Convent of St. Bernard, which, on being occupied by the light companies of the First regiment, was converted into a strong post by Saltoun, who was, of course, in command there. If the French intended to destroy the bridge of boats they would first need to retake the convent which made its security essential. The advance of the left column, consisting of the Second Brigade of Guards, was also successful, but the centre, driving towards St. Etienne, met with more serious opposition, though eventually the French were driven into the citadel, having lost one of their guns.

During March, Hope prepared for an assault on the fortifications, but no heavy artillery arrived to enable him to complete the task. The achievements of Wellington's army were all the more remarkable since it was perennially short of materiel and of artillery in particular. This fact made the most careful planning for engagements essential, but assaults on fortified positions were ever problematic to impossible. No fault can be laid at the feet of the artillerymen themselves, but the Board of Ordnance at home had much to answer for. Meanwhile, at Bayonne the infantry 'dug in'. Every house had to be turned into an entrenched post, which was the more necessary since the accuracy of the French gunners within the fort meant no sentry could expose himself to their view without attracting a potentially fatal shot.

As the populace of Bordeaux and its environs, a little over 100 miles to the north, had by this time declared their support for the Bourbon monarchy, Wellington, on the 8th of March, ordered Beresford to march a force to occupy the city, which he entered on the 12th of March. After remaining there a few days, Beresford left Lord Dalhousie in the city with the Seventh Division, and rejoined Wellington on the 18th.

The early stages of sieges tend to be dull for soldiers and by the middle of March Saltoun's period of intense activity had slowed markedly. Furthermore, his own post was now within St. Bernard's Convent which although substantially in ruins, nevertheless still offered a dry place to work, write and sleep. So, his relaxed letter to Catharine Thurlow is longer than its immediate predecessors and typically well informed.

St. Bernard's Convent,
March 13th, 1814.

I wrote you last week, my dear Miss Thurlow, from Beaucotte (Boucant), a small village in the rear of this place, and the day after we advanced and drove the enemy's posts into Bayonne and the citadel, and since that time we have been perfectly quiet on our part, and have the place closely invested, waiting for orders to besiege it, which have not as yet arrived from Lord Wellington, nor is it certain whether we are to besiege or not. I have the command of this post, which forms the right of the line on this side the river, and is close in with the citadel and dockyard, our advanced posts being about six hundred yards from them; it is on the high road from Bayonne to Beaucotte and the mouth of the Adour.

My mansion has a fine name, but is not very remarkable for accommodation. It was formerly a convent, and was *abimé* during the revolution, and the ladies turned adrift. Since that period, it has been made use of as a glass-house, but for want of trade they went to rack, and since we have taken possession the enemy have destroyed by shot and shell the small part of the house that was habitable, except the kitchen, in which I am now writing, which it will puzzle them to throw anything into; indeed for some days past they have left off firing at us, finding, I suppose, that they did us no harm.

I have no news of any sort or kind to tell you, as before you receive this you will have seen the account of Lord Wellington's victory over Soult, since which time he has been in cantonments in front of Mont Maman, and perfectly quiet. He was wounded slightly in the hip, and has been confined a few days in consequence. Soult has since the action received a reinforcement of nine thousand men from Suchet's army, which has retired from Catalonia, and we therefore expect soon to hear of another action if Soult should think himself strong enough to attack. In the meantime, all the reports that we get through France are of a pacific nature; indeed, they go so far as to say that the line of demarcation to be observed by the armies during the armistice is now being settled, but I rather think that this statement is premature.

The French people are heartily sick of the war, and if they could have peace, do not care whether Napoleon or a Bourbon is their king. They all seem to look towards the latter, as they say they never can have a permanent peace as long as Napoleon lives, but they are too much afraid of him to rise, as in case of failure they know he would revenge himself most properly; and as there is nothing left in the country but old men, they like to look twice before they leap. Let what will happen it cannot be long before I see you in No. 10, so for the present *adios*, my dear Miss Thurlow, and believe me ever yours,

Saltoun.

Very little of note occurred at Bayonne though it remained a dangerous place to be for the unwary. Those without the walls kept their heads down whenever possible and those within the walls did much the same. Opposing armies in close proximity to each other resort to sniping, though usually, if their situation continues, jointly prudently prefer to be provocative as little as possible. Time ultimately, of course, was on the side of the British for 30,000 men were waiting to take Bayonne whilst Soult had withdrawn his army, in effect leaving the garrison to its fate.

Saltoun remained ensconced behind the walls of his abandoned convent outpost. Although we do not have Catharine Thurlow's letters to Saltoun, it is clear from his reply to her in the following letter that (as expected) the news that he had decided to stay in the field and had not discussed his decision was not sitting well with her and she had, furthermore, made her feelings known to him. Saltoun's letter appears to contain elements of one side of a spat between two people who had acknowledged that they were now a 'couple'. Here we see Saltoun quite on the defensive, giving a reasonable account of himself (if in a deliberately over-complicated way given his situation was exactly what he had wanted), though it would be interesting to know Catharine's reaction to his rather patronising, 'my dear girl'.

St. Bernard's, before Bayonne,
20 March 1814.

Your letter of the 1st instant I received yesterday, and as this is our post-day I do not like putting off answering it till next week, so have got up very early this morning, or rather have not lain down again, for I am obliged now to turn out every morning before daylight, in order to see as soon as day breaks if the bold Frenchman has made any alteration in his lines or not, and to report accordingly.

You seem to think that I meant to have remained in this country had I got my promotion under any circumstances, and therefore of course think it odd I did not tell you so when I was in England last year; but, my dear girl, that event depended so much upon a contingency, that, although I thought it might happen, I certainly did not think it very likely, which I will explain to you as shortly as I can.

When I was in England I knew very well that some sort of arrangement was in contemplation by which the Guards would get promotion, either by taking our generals off the strength of the regiments as captains and giving their companies to the senior officers, letting them receive the pay and giving us the rank, or by removing them entirely from the regiment and giving them a specific pay equivalent to what they now receive.

Either of these things taking place would have made a number of us captains at the same time, and as most of them would have gone to England, there would have been a sufficient number in London to have done the duty without me; but by far the most probable thing at time was, that I, from being first for purchase, should got my promotion by purchase, before any arrangement of this kind could be settled, in which case I should have been the only officer promoted at the time, and must have gone home in my turn to do the duty in London, and have gone to Holland, or come out here again in the regular course of things. Now there could be no use in mentioning a thing which might never take place, and indeed which never has, at least not yet, and was not at all likely to happen in my case; but the circumstance of the augmentation taking place, which never came into anybody's head, put me exactly in the same situation as had the first happened, by promoting Reeve and Thomas at the same time as myself, and enabling me to remain, which I am glad to find you approve of, and I hope will be satisfied as to the explanation. What a lot of paper it has taken up, but I could not do it in fewer words. If I have many more military points to discuss, I shall make an officer of you by the time you thoroughly understand the different forms of speech.

Everything remains in the same state as when I wrote you last week, and as yet nobody can guess whether we are to besiege the place or not. Our casualties are very trifling. One of my men got cut in two the other day on sentry by a cannon-shot, and his comrade made the following epitaph on him:—

On sentry I fell a sacrifice
In cold blood to French cowardice;
Close to my head a cannon-ball you see,
Resembling that which was the death of me.

Not so bad for a private soldier. It is a most cowardly thing the way they fire at the sentries, as we have orders at present not to return fire on any account, and the rascals come up within pistol-shot of our sentries, at the same time that they are practising their recruits in firing at them from the works; but when our guns come up, by God we will make them look sharp enough after themselves.

Bordeaux has declared for the Bourbon, and we expect the whole of this part of the country to follow the example; so Boney must look sharp. I shall see you sooner than you seem to expect in your letter, and till then must content myself with writing.

Adieu, my dear Miss Thurlow, and believe me ever yours,

Saltoun.

As it transpired, the French did not have it all their own way when it came to sniping at sentries as Rees Gronow recalled in his reminiscences. One day when he was on outpost duty, he heard several shots coming from the same location within the French position. His captain, Grant, as the senior officer on duty arrived upon the scene to enquire why it was the enemy pickets were firing and he instructed Gronow to make his way to the front to discover what was happening. The following is recounted in Gronow's own words:

> Having arrived at the ravine which separated us from the French, I stumbled upon an advanced sentry, a German, who was coolly smoking his pipe. I asked whether the shots that had been heard came from his neighbourhood upon which he replied in broken English, *"Yes, zir, that feelow you see yonder has fired nine times at mine target,* (meaning his body) *but has missed. I hopes you, capitaine, will let me have one shot at him"*. The distance between the French picket and ours could not have been less than four hundred yards; so, without giving myself time to think I said: "Yes, you can have one shot at him". He levelled his musket (which, most notably, was a Brown Bess), fired and killed his man, whereupon, a sergeant and two or three soldiers who had seen him fall, ran down to the front and removed the body.

.

www.ingramcontent.com/pod-product-compliance
Lightning Source LLC
Chambersburg PA
CBHW032050080426
42733CB00006B/219